LEADING YOUR SALES TEAM

JIM PANCERO

DARTNELL is a publisher serving the world of business with books, manuals, newsletters and bulletins, and training materials for executives, managers, supervisors, salespeople, financial officials, personnel executives, and office employees. Dartnell also produces management and sales training videos and audiocassettes, publishes many useful business forms, and many of its materials and films are available in languages other than English. Dartnell, established in 1917, serves the world's business community. For details, catalogs, and product information, write to:

THE DARTNELL CORPORATION,
4660 N Ravenswood Ave,
Chicago, IL 60640-4595, U.S.A.
or phone (800) 621-5463, in U.S. and Canada.

Dartnell Training Limited
125 High Holborn
London, England
WC1V 6QA
or phone 011-44-071-404-1585

This publication is designed to provide accurate and authoritative information in regard to the subject matter covered. It is sold with the understanding that the publisher is not engaged in rendering legal, accounting, or other professional service. If legal advice or other expert assistance is required, the services of a competent professional person should be sought.

> — From a Declaration of Principles jointly adopted by a Committee of the American Bar Association and a Committee of Publishers.

Copyright 1995
Jim Pancero

ISBN 0-85013-200-2
Library of Congress Catalog Card Number: 94-068813

Printed in the United States of America by the Dartnell Press, Chicago, IL, 60640-4595

DEDICATION

This book is dedicated to my wife, Cyndie, and daughter, Kate,
the two most important people in my life.

About the Author

Jim Pancero is president of Jim Pancero, Inc., a sales and persuasion consulting firm in Cincinnati. Consulting on the subjects of sales management, advanced skills, and strategic corporate positioning, Jim has worked with more than 400 corporations in 60 different industries. His clients include AT&T, General Electric, Dun & Bradstreet, Wilson Sporting Goods, and Yellow Freight Systems.

Holding master's degrees in management and marketing, Jim has taught undergraduate and graduate business programs at several universities. He has more than 20 years of consumer and industrial sales and sales training experience. He is also the author of the audiocassette programs, *Selling at the Top* and *Leading the Team*, released by The Dartnell Corporation.

ACKNOWLEDGMENTS

There are many significant phases we all go through in our lives that help us change, grow, and achieve. In each of these phases, individuals with more experience, insight, or awareness help us learn and guide our journey. For me, there are a few who have been important mentors in my life.

Growing up in Cincinnati, I had what has become a rather unusual experience — a normal and loving childhood. My mother and father instilled in me an energy and drive that has never waned.

During high school, my father introduced my brother and me to a boys' organization called DeMolay. My years in DeMolay and the adult advisors who volunteered their time taught me leadership and how to be comfortable speaking in front of others, which has become the basis of my speaking and training career.

In 1974, during my first day of graduate school at the University of Cincinnati, I met Bill McGrane. As a self-esteem consultant, Bill opened a new world of personality and behavioral awareness, persuasiveness, and a true comfort with myself and all I could be. His impact on my view of life was profound. Several of the ideas he helped me understand are covered in this book.

As a consultant, trainer, and professional speaker since 1982, I have had the opportunity to meet an amazing group of experts, motivators, and true eccentrics. An important resource and an emotional anchor comes from my friends and fellow members at the National Speakers Association.

Training, speaking, and traveling around the world demands a unique blend of discipline, commitment, and passion. I could not survive all this were it not for my loving wife, Cyndie, and our daughter, Kate. Thank you for loving me and allowing me to pursue and enjoy my dreams.

CONTENTS

PREFACE

A s I travel around the country speaking and training, the experienced sales managers I meet all seem to be wrestling with the same problems. The majority have a solid understanding of how to sell but feel uncomfortable with and unaware of how they can be productive and effective coaches to their salespeople. Most of them became — or are about to become — sales managers because they outsold all the other salespeople within their organizations. Those of us in the selling industry have perpetuated a myth that success as a salesperson is based on eventually being promoted to sales manager. If we are really successful, the myth continues, we will ultimately be promoted to vice president of sales. Does this sound like the goal you have focused on in your selling career?

This myth of "selling success is achieved as a sales manager" is especially emphasized in our college business programs. In college, if you want to focus on a business degree, you have only a few choices of majors, like business administration, marketing, accounting, and finance. Why is there no major in selling? As a sales consultant and professional speaker, I have talked to a number of university business classes about selling and sales management. During my programs, I ask for anyone who plans to be a salesperson when they graduate to raise their hands. Consistently, less than ten percent of business majors respond. This is particularly interesting when you consider that several studies have shown that over 75 percent of all marketing and business administration majors wind up in a sales position as their first job. When I ask the rest of the class what they want to be when they graduate, most of them say they want to be managers. Our colleges are training business majors how to be real "successes" by teaching them how to be managers instead of teaching them how to achieve that goal by first becoming successful salespeople.

So, why do (did) you want to be a sales manager? The answer is different for each of us. But there are many individuals currently working as sales managers who have decided they do not enjoy management and want to return to full-time selling careers. One study reported that approximately half of all individuals who become sales managers eventually choose to go back to full-time selling. Success as a salesperson is based on what you personally accomplish by applying your intelligence, creativity, experience, and hard work; success as a sales manager is based on your ability to manage and coach others — two completely different sets of skills.

Once you become a sales manager, how much training are you likely to receive? The vast majority of sales managers receive no training on how to manage their people. There is an unspoken assumption that if you are successful as an independent salesperson, you will, of course, also be a successful sales manager. Even though the skills required for each position is completely different, the assumption is that a great salesperson will naturally make a great sales manager.

So, how do you become a great sales manager? Success as a sales manager is based on three major skills: awareness, proactive prioritization, and coaching.

AWARENESS

How aware are you of what your job really involves? A sales manager's job is not to sell, but to manage others who sell. Sales managers ineffectively focus a large percentage of their time either on their own accounts or on becoming directly involved in personally selling their sales reps' customers.

This book is divided into two parts. Each covers one of the two most critical jobs of sales management. Part I discusses how to effectively manage and motivate your people. Part II teaches you to manage the selling process successfully. Do you understand the skills necessary to manage and motivate your people? How effective are you at helping your people see the big picture of the overall selling process? This book discusses both of these major skill areas.

PROACTIVE PRIORITIZATION

Just increasing your awareness is not enough to increase your success as a sales manager. You also need to increase your ability to proactively prioritize and to say no to ineffective information and activity requests. All sales managers are significantly overworked; they have demands for their time and attention that they can never fulfill. Let's face it, as a sales manager, your desk will never be completely clean, and you will never sit around trying to figure out what you can do to keep busy.

Are you going to proactively prioritize your focus and work efforts, or are you going to reactively allow others to choose what gets your attention? Most newer sales managers find their environment controls them instead of them controlling and leading their environment. Throughout this book, we discuss ways to build a stronger proactive focus for prioritizing your efforts as a successful sales manager.

COACHING

Are you comfortable guiding others toward increased success? Effective managers not only need to increase their own awareness and prioritization skills, but those of their salespeople as well. Understanding and dealing with the emotions and varying behaviors of others is one of the most difficult, yet critical, components of successful sales management.

What is a sales manager's job? How you verbally answer this question is not as relevant as how your actions answer it. Most sales managers' actions reactively define their job as making sure all their people are performing above a certain minimum level. In this book, we take a more proactive position by defining a sales manager's job as the ability to help all salespeople achieve more than they would on their own.

Let's assume you have three people reporting to you. One consistently outperforms the assigned sales quota, one performs acceptably, and one significantly underperforms in several key areas that are affecting both sales volumes and customer satisfaction. Which of these three will get the majority of your attention? If you are like most sales managers, you will ignore your top performer, pay some attention to your average performer to try to get him or her "fired up," and focus most of your energy on the person who produces the least total revenue. The goal of this book is to help establish a balance in which everyone receives coaching that helps achieve a level of performance that would be impossible without ongoing coaching and insight. Your job is to help even your best performer improve his or her selling success and profitability.

Are you comfortable with the idea of helping each member of your sales team increase personal satisfaction and success as a professional salesperson? This book offers ideas and insights on how to increase your ability to coach and guide your best *and* worst performers.

READING IS THE EASY PART

Reading this book will be the easiest part of increasing your success as a sales manager. The hard part will be implementing these ideas, and the *hardest* part will be permanently incorporating the applicable ideas into your long-term managerial habits. How committed are you to changing and enhancing your current level of sales management skills? Everyone wants to change, but few are willing to change themselves to achieve their desired goals. What are you going to do to begin changing and improving your skills and personal style of management?

Each sales manager's work environment is different. If you work in a large corporation, you may be constrained by bureaucratic inflexibility and rigidity in changing any management process. If you own or work for a small independent company, you will undoubtedly be constrained by the lack of time and money available to implement the changes necessary to improve your overall selling environment. Since it is unlikely that anyone will be able to successfully implement all of the proven management ideas in this book, you need to decide what you can use within the existing constraints of your environment. The goal of this book is not to completely change your current environment, but to provide you with a level of personal awareness that will allow you to focus on the areas within your organization that you *can* change and improve.

How much change and improvement are you willing to fight for within your company? May you enjoy the process as you work to enhance the skills of your salespeople.

Jim Pancero

Sales and Sales Management Consulting

PART I

MANAGING AND MOTIVATING YOUR SALES FORCE

Throughout this book, we talk about sales managers' two main responsibilities: managing and motivating their salespeople, and managing the selling environment. The chapters in Part One are primarily concerned with the first of these responsibilities. Chapters 1 through 5 focus on identifying your management style, examining how your style affects your sales team's motivational environment, and suggesting ways to improve your management style and, in turn, your overall environment.

CHAPTER 1

FROM "DOING MANAGER" TO "MANAGING MANAGER"

A sales manager's job is not to sell, but to manage and motivate salespeople. The manager needs to lead the team's selling efforts so it continues to exceed its annual quotas and goals.

Does this sound like your job description? Are each of your salespeople meeting or exceeding their goals? As their manager, do you feel that you are driving them as hard as possible, but that your sales are still not growing as fast as they could? Do you feel like you are working at 120 percent capacity, but there is always more to accomplish?

In this chapter, we will discuss your job as a sales manager and how much time you really spend managing your people. We will explore how to evaluate your present responsibilities and how to begin the transition from "doing manager" to "managing manager."

SALES MANAGERS — THEN AND NOW

The '50s and '60s

In the 1950s and 1960s, a sales manager's job was to be the team leader. Becoming a sales manager was the top sales award given to the top salesperson in the company. The executive view was that only the best salespeople would make the best sales managers. If you outsold everyone else, you were automatically expected — as sales manager — to know how to make your team sell as well as you did.

The key sales management phrase of this era was, "Let's go out today and close some business!" A sales manager's key function was to ride with each sales representative as often as possible. The manager acted like a drill sergeant, constantly whipping his salespeople into shape. The best salespeople were verbally "pumped up," whereas the worst ones were "beaten up." The manager was also expected to be a product expert, solving all product problems his salespeople could not solve on their own. Many present-day sales managers, who claim to be excellent coaches and team leaders, still subscribe to this outdated management style. Their basic question to their salespeople is, "What did you close today?" Let's consider what a negative effect such methods can have on your people.

Most salespeople feel they are working as hard as they can and are committed to their jobs and their companies. It is critical to remember this, even if you think they could be working harder. If you were a salesperson and felt you were already working at maximum capacity, how would you feel if your manager tried to give you a motivational, "pump you up" speech whenever he or she rode with you? The implied message is that your manager does not believe you are working at maximum capacity.

The '70s

The sales manager's job changed in the 1970s. Most companies began to realize that yelling at and pumping up their salespeople was not increasing sales, so sales managers reentered the selling process to "help out." The emphasis was for the sales manager to be the top salesperson. A successful sales manager led by example, normally carrying the toughest or largest accounts. Most likely, he or she was also the most senior sales professional in the company.

An example of this type of management was seen in a Canadian forms company whose vice president of sales, Shawn, was responsible for managing 12 salespeople in addition to two accounts that generated over one million dollars a year in sales. Shawn had no time for his people; he was too busy making money for the company. The salespeople could not go to him for any help — a serious detriment since several of them were newer and less experienced employees. As a result, the team did not make its quota, and two of the rookie salespeople quit in frustration.

The '80s

The 1980s brought another change when companies realized that selling and sales management had become much more complex and now needed the attention of a full-time sales manager. The manager's job became more refined and demanding as it shifted from being out in the field with the salespeople to remaining in the central office and providing help when needed. In reality, most sales managers still carried their own accounts, but their selling efforts were seen as more of a necessity or a personal security blanket than a critical contribution to the job itself.

A number of assumptions were driving this "new" methodology. One was that sales managers were good enough to manage both their own sales territory and their salespeople. A manager offered support and solutions to salespeople's corporate and customer problems. This made the manager's position completely reactive; a salesperson had to ask for help before the sales manager became involved with his or her efforts.

Another assumption was that salespeople knew how to sell and did not require the intensive supervision and discipline prevalent in the '50s and '60s. Problems were expected to result from interdepartmental issues and corporate bureaucracy.

Motivating the sales force was based on the assumption that the only things salespeople wanted and needed from their managers were help in problem solving and the ability to run corporate interference. Although there was still an occasional motivational pep talk at regular sales meetings, the sales manager's major contribution to the team was to remove all the day-to-day obstacles to success that his or her salespeople faced.

The idea at the time was to give a great deal of attention to the top performers and to ignore the underachievers, making the underachievers crave their sales manager's attention. This desire would supposedly motivate them to improve their selling efforts so they too could gain recognition.

The '90s

A tremendous number of companies still use the management styles established in the 1970s and 1980s. Their sales managers do not ride with salespeople on a regular basis and may go months without spending time in a sales territory. These managers are so busy selling to their own accounts or fighting internal corporate fires that they have completely lost contact with their customers' daily problems and concerns.

When was the last time you sat down with one of your salespeople and helped him or her work out a strategy for an important account? How much time do you spend riding with your salespeople, coaching and counseling them on sales calls, and interacting with their customers as the sales manager?

The answers to these questions are determined by your style of management and your priorities as a manager. The next section looks at different types of sales managers. Let's explore what type of manager you are and what style will help you achieve the greatest success.

THE THREE LEVELS OF RESPONSIBILITY

The first step is to identify how much time you actually spend managing your salespeople. To do this, you need to evaluate your job position and responsibilities. What do you do?

There are three levels of responsibility in every company:

- *Doer.* This person has only one responsibility: to do the job. One example of a doer is a salesperson who is responsible for selling in an assigned territory. Doers are evaluated and compensated based only on how productive and successful they are in accomplishing their assigned tasks.

- *Doing manager.* This person is responsible both for his or her personal performance and for managing others. A shop foreman in a production facility is considered a doing manager. He or she is held accountable for a specific level of work and for making sure that other members of his or her team also produce at acceptable levels.

- *Managing manager.* This person concentrates solely on managing others' work. Managing managers are not assigned personal production expectations; their only concern is to ensure that the members of their team accomplish *their* assigned activities. A managing manager's performance is only as good as the total team's performance.

Which of these job descriptions fits you? Are you a doer, a doing manager, or a managing manager? The answer can make a big difference in the way you do your job.

John, a sales manager for a medical supply company, functions as a doing manager. He not only has five experienced salespeople reporting directly to him; he carries six of the largest and most important company accounts. John is constantly overloaded. Problems with his large accounts always seem to require his attention just when one or two of his salespeople most need help with their accounts.

Does this situation sound familiar? Are you a doing sales manager? Do you carry your own sales accounts in addition to your management responsibilities?

Compare John's circumstances to those of a managing manager. Maureen is a sales manager for a pharmaceuticals manufacturer with 12 salespeople reporting to her. Four of her people have little or no sales experience, and she structures her time to provide more training and support for them. She is available to all the representatives to help them with strategic planning and problem solving, and she rides with each of them on a regular basis to coach their efforts and get their feedback on how their jobs are going. As a managing manager, Maureen has no accounts of her own; her entire focus is on the efforts and improvement of her sales team.

Unlike Maureen, most doing sales managers have to continually select which side of their job will suffer. Is it better to put more time into your own territory this month and let your salespeople go without your help and guidance? Or is it better to pay more attention to your team's accounts and problems and let your personal territory slide? It is a continual, and certainly not uncommon, crisis.

In reality, the majority of sales managers are currently functioning as doing managers. Most of them carry personal accounts because they (or their managers) want the added responsibility. They give several reasons for this, which are mostly based on the sales manager's (or executive manager's) lack of awareness. The following sections look at these reasons and the truth or fallacy behind each.

Augmenting a Small Sales Staff

Some companies simply do not have enough sales staff to financially justify a full-time managing sales manager. Because the company is so small, the sales manager's hands-on contribution to sales efforts is critical to the company's bottom line. For example, Brad, a sales manager with a large manufacturer that had only one sales division, led a sales team consisting of only two fairly experienced salespeople. Brad was unhappy because he had to carry several large accounts in addition to managing his people. He felt that he was not really a manager because he spent so much time selling, and that he could make a greater contribution to the company if he got rid of his accounts and became a "real" sales manager. However, given the small number of salespeople and their level of experience, there was not enough managerial work to keep Brad busy full time. Also, his personal selling efforts contributed to good sales increases in the sales division.

As this example shows, you may need to be a doing manager if there are only a few people reporting to you.

Staying Current with the Industry

Although a small sales staff may require you to work as a doing manager, a large number of sales managers have sufficient staff to warrant being full-time managing managers. Many of them will say, "Selling my own accounts lets me know what's happening in the industry." But is this statement true?

Assume that you now spend 25 percent of your time selling to your own accounts. Will you gain a stronger awareness of your customers and market by selling personally to a few large accounts? Or will you gain a stronger awareness riding with each of your salespeople and talking with most of your customers? Experienced sales managers consistently maintain that you will learn more by talking with many customers on a continual basis than you can by working with just a few accounts.

Impressing Your Salespeople

Another frequent rationale given by doing sales managers is, "Carrying my own accounts lets me show my people I know I'm still the best salesperson, so they'll respect me more as a manager." As we discussed earlier, if you are a doing manager, your obligations to your personal accounts often take priority over coaching and leading your salespeople. Although they may respect your sales abilities, the frustration caused by your lack of leadership will not create respect for your managerial skills. There is also a question as to whether your team members will learn more about selling from your example (the old 1970s approach) or from having you along on sales calls to provide support and suggestions.

Keeping a Hand in the Selling Process

Even though personally handling accounts does not generate an effective return on their time, a strong percentage of doing sales managers carry accounts simply because they seem uncomfortable with the idea of not selling. They may say, "Carrying my own accounts lets me keep my hand in the real selling process so I can be a better coach to my people." The key question here, as with the idea of staying current with the industry, is whether you will help your people more by focusing on the details of a few personal accounts or from exposing yourself to a greater variety of experiences attained through riding with and talking to your entire sales team.

Justifying Performance

Many sales managers earned their positions by being one of the top sales-people. Because their definition of success is based on personal sales volume, they find it hard to let go of accounts, even though they are overworked. They are reluctant to act as full-time managing managers because they fear their executive managers will no longer see how they are contributing to the company.

They may be right. Many performance appraisals give greater weight to numbers than to managerial performance, forcing sales managers to remain in their less effective doing manager roles. An example of this may be seen in the trust department of one commercial bank. Senior management wanted the trust officers to become more sales-oriented and the trust department's total revenues to increase. Jack, the vice president in charge of personal trust, and the two senior managers reporting to him were each personally carrying a full load of trust accounts. This was a large bank, employing 75 personal trust officers with varying degrees of experience, all of whom reported to these three managers. The managers, however, were so busy with their own accounts that collectively they spent less than ten hours a week on the problems and issues presented by the 75 trust officers under them. Although in strategic planning sessions, Jack and his two managers agreed they would have to give up their accounts to meet the department's goals, six months later they were all still carrying 90 percent of their original account loads.

The reason for this was the bank's overemphasis on semi-annual performance appraisals. The senior managers' appraisals focused on how they had personally managed important accounts, and their actual managerial activities were given little importance or attention. Only after their written performance plans were altered and the head of trust met with each of them to confirm that the evaluation system would change, did these three managers release their accounts and begin functioning as full-time managing managers.

This behavior is not uncommon. Look at your own situation. How did you prove to your senior management that you could be a successful sales manager? Was it your selling accomplishments? Your talent for handling tough customer situations? Or was it your ability to organize and implement a special project? If you have spent your entire career as a doing salesperson, there is a good chance your definition of success is based on what you have personally accomplished.

MOVING FROM DOING TO MANAGING

The transition from doing manager to managing manager takes self-discipline and effort. Before you adjust to new or increased managerial responsibilities, you may need to convince others that this change is justified and necessary. The following are three of the most important issues in your shift to a full-time managerial role:

1. becoming comfortable with your new management responsibilities;
2. making sure your performance evaluation accurately reflects your job requirements; and
3. gaining your manager's support for your new role.

Building Your Comfort Level
A major component of your success as a sales manager will be based on how comfortable and stable you feel in your job. The more time you spend

worrying about your own performance, the less energy you will have to direct and support your team's efforts. The following are some ideas to help you feel more at ease as a managing manager:

- Check with your local chamber of commerce or public library to see if there are any sales management organizations in your area. Becoming active in this type of group can give you the opportunity to network and receive advice from more experienced sales managers.

- If no groups are available, look for a more experienced sales manager who will agree to act as your mentor — a private coach who will meet with you on a regular basis to offer coaching assistance, guidance, and moral support.

- If you are comfortable in your relationship with your manager, ask him or her for help or a recommendation of where to go for help. If you work for a large corporation, your human resources department may also have some suggestions.

- Consider joining (or creating) a monthly breakfast or lunch group of four or five sales management colleagues. This informal group meets to share experiences and suggestions. Most groups have members from a variety of companies and industries.

Addressing Evaluation Concerns

Successful sales managers are comfortable with measuring their success based solely on the productive efforts of the people reporting to them. How do you feel about being evaluated on your team's efforts rather than on your own? The more you move from being a doing manager to a managing manager, the more difficult it will be to prove exactly what you did over the past year. Are you ready for this challenge?

Gaining Manager Support

What can you do to ensure your manager agrees with your efforts and direction? What happens if you are comfortable being a managing manager, but your manager still wants you to carry accounts?

Begin by talking to your executive management about how you could increase your effectiveness and the total success of your sales team by

---

TEAM LEADER'S TOOL

BECOMING A MANAGING MANAGER

Start planning the steps you need to take to become a more effective managing manager.

1. List all of the accounts you now handle.
2. Clarify the real reasons you are still carrying them.
3. Identify who can best take over these accounts for you.
4. How can this transition be handled smoothly? List specific steps.
5. Use the blank forms on pages 212 and 213 of the Appendix to begin working on the staff development plan you will discuss with your manager. Determine a timetable for securing your manager's approval of your plan.
6. Establish the date you will present your staff development plan to your manager.
7. List sales management groups you can contact (name, contact person, phone number, and dates and locations of meetings).
8. List the reasons for you to become a full-time managing manager.
9. Establish your target date for becoming a managing manager.

---

devoting 100 percent of your time to managing and helping your salespeople. To illustrate your point, keep a diary for a few months and log where and how you spend your time each day. Consider breaking your time down into the following categories:

- selling and supporting your own accounts;
- coaching and training your sales team;
- resolving problems;
- attending internal meetings and discussions; and
- completing paperwork.

The idea is to get a better understanding of exactly how your time is allocated. Also keep track of any conflicts, such as when you have a problem in your own account at the same time one of your people needs assistance.

After you have collected this information, sit down with your manager and discuss how and where you are spending your time. Identify the skills each of your salespeople need to improve to enhance their overall performance. Emphasize the benefits of allowing you to invest more time in working with these people. Prove that by maintaining your accounts you are costing the company revenue that could otherwise be employed in improving your team's sales. You will also need to explain how your accounts can be reassigned to and supported by other members of the team. Show how you plan to turn the accounts over without disrupting revenues. Emphasize that you will still be involved with the accounts, but on a managerial level.

If you are not currently working with your salespeople as a coach and a leader, you are probably still most productive in working on your own accounts. You may need to hone your coaching skills and use them to boost your team's performance before talking to your manager about transferring your accounts and devoting all of your efforts to leadership activities.

A Final Word on Practicality

If you, and not your manager, are the only reason you are still carrying accounts, ask yourself, "What is the best use of my expertise?" Most sales managers are wasting their true contribution to their company by focusing only on their own selling efforts. Every salesperson can benefit from increased manager involvement on a regular basis.

There are instances, however, when carrying your own accounts may be a positive action or a short-term necessity. Consider one company that sells large manufacturing equipment used on assembly lines. The national sales manager took personal responsibility for one account, her major motivations being travel cost containment and convenience. The account was headquartered in Boston, where she lived, and the closest sales representative lived over 200 miles away. The manager felt that because of her proximity, she could provide a higher level of service for the account. (It also allowed her to spend less time traveling and more time with her family.)

Are there good reasons for you to continue to handle one or more accounts as a sales manager? Sometimes this is a difficult decision to make. The determining factor, however, should always be what the final impact on your company will be if you continue to carry accounts instead of becoming a managing manager.

SUMMARY

In most cases, your company will profit most from using you as a managing manager rather than as a doing manager. It is up to you to provide financial justification for transferring your remaining accounts and focusing exclusively on managing and coaching others' efforts. By clearly demonstrating that maintaining your accounts is costing your company revenue, you can free yourself to invest more time in increasing the selling skills of your salespeople.

One of the major challenges you face as a sales manager in today's competitive business environment is the need for a tougher, more aggressive approach to winning business. The philosophy of helping only when you are asked is not appropriate when business conditions, competitive pressures, and customer demands are changing faster than the average salesperson can keep up with. How fast has your industry changed in this competitive environment? More importantly, what have you done, as a sales manager, to help your people deal with all their new competitive pressures? In Chapter 2, we look at ways of meeting these challenges in a proactive manner.

EXHIBIT 1.1 SALES TEAM DEVELOPMENT PLAN

Overall goals for your sales team in the next 12 months:

_____

_____

_____

_____

_____

_____

_____

Specific training you will give team members to help them achieve these goals and improve their overall performance:

_____

_____

_____

_____

Your team's goals and objectives for the next five years:

_____

_____

_____

_____

Percentage growth in performance each team member will need to achieve these goals five years from now:

_____   _____%

_____   _____%

_____   _____%

_____   _____%

_____   _____%

_____   _____%

EXHIBIT 1.2 SALESPERSON GROWTH AND DEVELOPMENT PLAN

Salesperson: _____

Strengths: _____

_____

_____

_____

_____

Areas that need improvement: _____

_____

_____

_____

_____

Action plan to help this person improve: _____

_____

_____

_____

_____

How you will measure this person's success and growth:_____

_____

_____

_____

_____

_____

CHAPTER 2

BECOMING A PROACTIVE MANAGER

Many sales managers still rely on strategies from the past, focusing their attention on internal matters or their own accounts and waiting for their salespeople to approach them with problems. Some even subscribe to the theory that only the top salespeople deserve management attention, ignoring the average and below-average achievers. Their overall management style is reactive rather than proactive and concentrates their efforts on a variety of tasks that are not necessarily helpful to the team's objectives as a whole.

A LEADERSHIP FOCUS

Today you need to concentrate on *leading* your people, not outselling them. Your success as a sales manager hinges on how consistently you provide these resources to your sales force: guidance, structure, and communication.

Guidance

The first factor of sales management success is how much guidance you give your salespeople. To do this, you need to be a coach and a strategist. You need to sit down privately with each of your salespeople on a regular basis to review and discuss their overall territory as well as their important accounts. Use the following questions to help you decide the issues you want to cover in these meetings:

- What are some possible solutions to the difficult competitive challenges they will most likely face on their next customer call?
- What accounts do they feel are nearest to being closed, and what will it take to close them?
- What do they plan to accomplish on their next sales call to their most important accounts?
- How will they handle any challenges to their pricing?
- Who are their toughest competitors for the same business, and how are they positioning their competitive uniqueness?

- How are you communicating and positioning your competitive message of uniqueness?

See Chapter 9 for details of how to redefine and reinforce your competitive uniqueness.

Your job as a sales manager is *not* to do your salespeoples' selling, but to help them see what they need to do next to increase their competitive advantage.

Structure

The second factor of sales management success is how much ongoing structure your salespeople develop. Most salespeople tend to be disorganized. You need to help them create systems that will (1) enhance their efficiency, and (2) ensure their selling efforts are focusing on a predetermined list of prioritized objectives. This means assisting them in setting up calendars and customer tracking systems, showing them how to manage paperwork, and helping them prioritize their information flows.

Communication

The third factor of sales management success is the quality of ongoing communication with your salespeople and how you involve them in the direction and focus of your business. You need to meet with them regularly to explain how their efforts tie in with your company's overall goals, strategies, and future. They need to be focused, energized, and directed toward your common objectives.

How much time and effort are you currently investing in each of these three areas of leadership? Most sales managers are too distracted by day-to-day operational issues to help their salespeople plan ongoing sales efforts. They don't have time to work with their people because they are too busy doing everything else. Minor issues and responsibilities absorb them, leaving them almost no time to address the truly important aspects of sales management.

Does this sound familiar? If so, you are not alone. Nor are you helpless to do anything about it. You can turn things around. The first step is to look at how you spend your time.

TIME ALLOCATION

In evaluating a sales manager's important responsibilities, we are able to identify two important proactive areas that are critical to success and a number of reactive secondary areas that tend to get in the way of strategic effectiveness.

As a sales manager, your two most critical responsibilities are motivating your people and guiding the selling process. Although this sounds obvious, if you are like most sales managers, you find it difficult to focus on these responsibilities because you are distracted by the day-to-day duties imposed by four reactive job responsibilities: personal selling time, "administrivia," crisis management, and other nonselling projects.

We examine each of these responsibilities and their effects on a manager's success in the following sections.

Personal Selling Time

As we discussed in Chapter 1, most doing managers spend between 25 and 50 percent of their time selling to their own accounts, and many managers who do not have assigned customer accounts still spend 20 to 50 percent of their time prospecting for new customers. If selling must be a part of your sales management job, prospecting is better than dealing with established accounts. With prospecting, you can delay or walk away from your own work if your salespeople need your help without significant long-term consequences. In either case, however, carrying a sales territory takes time away from your ability to manage and lead your people.

One of the goals of this book is to help you re-evaluate where you, as a sales manager, need to focus your time and energies. Although over 70 percent of sales managers spend a portion of their time selling, there are more productive ways to invest time and expertise to become proactive managing managers.

Administrivia

Administrivia is defined as the processing of paper for the sheer joy of processing paper. Of course, everyone needs to deal with paperwork — it is a mandatory part of any manager's job. But sales managers in the 1980s got so bogged down with documenting details, collecting information from other departments, and constructing a "paper trail" that they neglected the important managerial function of coaching their salespeople. Ask yourself the following questions to assess how much time you spend shuffling paper instead of working with your salespeople:

- Do you write memos when you could just as easily make a phone call?
- Do you ever delay working with one of your salespeople because you have too much paperwork to do or too many reports to complete?
- Have you ever written a "letter to the file"?
- How many hours each week do you spend on internal paperwork and reports?

In Chapter 8, we talk about how you can reduce and improve your information flows.

Crisis Management

The third reactive drain on your time is crisis management, or stepping in to solve crises instead of teaching your people effective methods so they can prevent or diffuse them. Although managing customer crises will always be an important part of any sales manager's job, it may be taking up an excessive and unnecessary amount of your time. Some sales managers spend so much time reacting to and solving crises, they have no time to prevent problems. When do you tend to get involved in your salesperson's crisis? Do you proactively get involved to help guide your people, or are you pulled in only after the crisis has blown up and you can only implement expensive damage control measures?

One of the major problems a large number of salespeople have with crisis management is knowing when to ask their managers for assistance. Because it is unclear when they should call for help, newer salespeople tend to ask too soon; more experienced representatives hold on to their problems too long. Both situations can create significant difficulties for the sales manager.

The rookie salesperson may present you with a new "crisis" every day, which can be a serious time drain if you allow it to continue. In such a situation, most sales managers eventually overreact and tell the salesperson to solve his or her own problems. The result of this action is that the salesperson sits on the next problem until it blows up into a real crisis without you even being aware that a problem exists.

Senior salespeople are inclined toward the other extreme and keep their problems to themselves until it is too late for you to have any positive impact. This comes from the training we have given them over the years: If they are really professional and good at their jobs, they will solve their own problems. Have you given your experienced people that kind of "solve your own problem" message?

The Four Stages of Crisis Management. We assume our people should know when to ask us to get involved in account problems, even though we have never explained how effective crisis management works. As shown in Exhibit 2.1, there are four stages to solving customer problems effectively. As we discuss these stages, remember that this process is meant as a management coaching guide.

The first stage of crisis management is when the salesperson handles the problem. He or she is able to resolve the situation successfully without involving or informing anyone else.[1]

If the salesperson is unable to solve the problem alone, he or she moves to the second stage by involving the sales manager as a coach or advisor. During this stage, the sales manager is only passively involved in the problem. The salesperson provides information and updates and receives advice and guidance from the sales manager. At this stage, it is unnecessary for the sales manager to speak with the customer directly. As far as the customer is concerned, the problem is still being handled by the salesperson.

---

[1] What constitutes a "successful" resolution to a problem? It must be an answer that is acceptable to both the company and the customer, resulting in a continued (profitable) relationship with that customer. Each situation is different and the degree of success depends on the level of compromise given by both sides. Based on what stage of crisis management the problem reaches, the salesperson, sales manager, or senior management must decide which actions will correct the problem and satisfy the customer without serious detriment to the company. Chapter 10 details the steps for coaching your salespeople in effective problem resolution.

How long should a salesperson work at a problem before progressing to the second stage? There is no right or wrong answer because each situation is different. The process is an intuitive one that requires experience and coaching to understand and successfully implement.

As a sales manager, it is critical for you to maintain an ongoing dialog with your people in their first years of selling. Rookies have no idea when a problem is too big for them to handle alone because they have no frame of reference. In working with newer people, you must help them identify when it is best to initiate the second phase of crisis management. It is also imperative that you discuss how they can handle this type of problem successfully the next time it occurs.

The majority of customer problems can be resolved effectively in either the first or second stages of crisis management. However, if it remains unresolved, it may be referred to as an account crisis and needs to move to the third stage. This is when the sales manager becomes actively involved. By this point the problem has most likely gotten so complex that the salesperson is only implementing the manager's instructions. As the lead person on this crisis, the sales manager is likely to seek the opinions and guidance of upper management.

If the problem is still unresolved, it now needs to move to the fourth and final stage of crisis management where senior or executive management becomes actively involved and takes over negotiations in a leadership role to solve the crisis. It is exceptionally rare that a problem progresses all the way to the fourth stage.

As a sales manager, you may find these four crisis management stages self-evident. The challenge is not your sales force's awareness of the stages, but knowing when it is proper and acceptable to move a problem to the next highest stage. Most salespeople learn by experience, from feedback received from past problems, when it is appropriate to move a problem to the next stage. For example, if five years ago Diane brought her manager a problem she felt needed to be moved to a higher stage and was reprimanded for not solving the problem herself, she learned that she was supposed to deal with all problems on her own — no matter what management may say now.

Instructing the Sales Force. How have you instructed your salespeople to handle their account problems? If you have not discussed this with them recently, how can they know when it is appropriate and essential to come to you for help and guidance? The following suggestions can help you clarify and improve your team members' timing for moving their problems to a higher stage:

1. Review the four stages of crisis management with your salespeople after each major problem is solved. Reinforce their action when they sought help appropriately or point out how they moved too slowly or too quickly in asking for management assistance.

2. Review successful resolutions to account problems with your sales team on a regular basis. In your sales meetings, show your people how a specific problem progressed through the various stages at the proper intervals. This can also be done in the form of a debriefing following the resolution of a major customer problem.

Only by walking your people through previous customer problems can you help them understand how to handle future situations successfully.

Example. One successful implementation of the four crisis management steps was achieved by an experienced salesperson at IBM.

A major commercial bank had one of IBM's largest computer systems installed in its data center. A foreign manufacturer of computer mainframes wanted to enter the U.S. market and began selling to the same bank. (A mainframe is the central processing unit that is the center of any large computer system. At the time, a large mainframe cost between $1 million and $2 million or leased for $30,000 a month.)

The lease on the bank's IBM mainframe was up for renewal within a few months. Dave, the senior IBM sales representative responsible for the account, discovered that the bank was seriously evaluating the foreign competitor. The competitor wanted to place its first U.S. system with a visible, conservative customer as a "showcase" account. Showcase accounts are sold at a significant discount with the stipulation that the vendor can then publicize the installation and offer prospective clients tours and demonstrations to prove the performance and reliability of the equipment.

Dave realized this problem was much too significant to handle on his own and immediately moved to the second stage of crisis management. Dave's manager instructed him to go back to the customer and learn as much as possible about the competitor's presentations and proposals.

After Dave gathered all available information, the problem was identified as being too big for the sales manager to deal with as a stage three crisis. Within a matter of days, the situation escalated to a stage four crisis, and a corporate team, comprised of experts on the competitor's systems, was called in to lead the sales effort. Although Dave and his sales manager were still involved, the situation was now led by an experienced executive team.

TEAM LEADER'S TOOL

PROVIDING CRISIS FEEDBACK

To prevent problems from reaching stage four, give your people ongoing feedback every time they handle a problem.

- Review the four stages of crisis management with your salesperson after each problem is resolved.
- If he or she was right to bump the problem up to the next stage, reinforce that decision with positive comments.
- If he or she asked for assistance too soon or too late, point out alternative actions.
- Set aside time in your sales meetings to review successful resolutions to customer problems. Tell how the problem progressed through the various stages with the proper timing.
- When you deal with a new salesperson's customer problems, be sure to discuss how he or she can handle this type of problem successfully in the future.

After numerous meetings and customer presentations, it was clear that the competitor's final offer would save the bank over $1 million during the life of its lease. IBM lost the bank to the foreign manufacturer, but the management team made a point of publicly congratulating Dave for such an excellent effort. Although the company was disappointed at losing business, management appreciated Dave's efficient handling of the situation. He knew when to ask for help, and he stayed involved to help evaluate and present solutions. Because Dave and his sales manager understood crisis management and when to ask for help, the executive management team had the opportunity to try to save the account.

Other Nonselling Projects

The fourth reactive drain on your time as a sales manager is the time spent on all the special projects you get pulled into. In most companies, the sales management team is an easy target for the "exception" projects that come along. When someone is needed to chair the annual United Way fund drive, manage the company picnic, or head up the local college campus volunteer project, a sales manager tends to end up with the assignment. There is a bias in most companies that every other manager is busier than the sales manager. Since most people do not even understand what sales managers do, giving them one more small assignment does not seem like a problem.

How many "special projects" or nonsales-related committees have you been "volunteered for" during the past year? As a sales manager, one of the skills you need to develop is the ability to say "no." In selling, we are taught to say "yes" to customers whenever possible, and this desire to satisfy others often carries over into our sales management positions. As a sales manager, you need to be a monomaniac, agreeing to work only on projects or activities that directly affect your job and that will help you achieve your goals. When you must refuse a request to help, list the reasons why the project would be better done by someone else, with an emphasis on the effect such an assignment would have on the sales force.

Evaluating Time Spent

With all the reactive diversions and distractions, you may spend almost no time motivating and managing your people and the selling process — even though these are the only areas you can influence that will actually increase your sales. Is it possible to achieve a fifty/fifty balance in which you spend half your time managing and motivating your people and the other half managing the selling process? Probably not. But it is possible to increase the amount of time you spend doing each of these proactive tasks.

First, you need to find out where your time is going now. If you have not already started to track your time, use the evaluation form in Exhibit 2.2 now. The first day's log has been filled out as an example; a blank form is provided in Appendix A. To help you see what is keeping you from managing and motivating your people, your time log includes a category for each of the four reactive responsibilities. The following questions can help you identify the areas where your time is spent:

- **Managing and motivating your people.** How many performance discussions do you initiate? How often do you sit down with your people one-on-one and ask them about their job? How often do you solicit their opinions about you, your company, your products, and customers?

- **Managing the selling process.** How much time do you spend coaching your people on problem accounts? How many times do you offer strategic suggestions on an important account? Do you help your people plan out their next sales calls on their important accounts? Do you ride with one or more of your people on a weekly basis? Do you use one-on-one time for proactive coaching and account strategy discussions?

- **Personal account selling.** How much time do you spend handling your own accounts?

- **Administrivia.** How much time do you spend on general paperwork, forecasts, and meetings, especially paperwork that benefits another internal department but does not offer any benefit to your customers?

- **Crisis management.** How much time do you spend dealing with product delivery problems, angry customers' invoicing problems, or exception pricing?

- **Other projects.** How many projects have you worked on because you wanted to help out (or they were assigned to you) and then found they interfered with your ability to manage your salespeople and the selling process?

After keeping track of your time in each of these areas for one week, use the first blank column in Exhibit 2.3 to break down the results. Now think about how much time you would spend on each of these activities as a managing manager. Enter these percentages in the last column of the exhibit and compare them to your real time allocation. How would you like to be spending your time? What changes are you willing to make to achieve your goals?

The final evaluation of how you can use your time successfully is based on the operational, tactical, and strategic management and selling issues discussed in the next section.

SHIFTING FROM REACTIVE TO PROACTIVE MANAGEMENT

There are three areas you need to focus on to be a successful manager.

- *Operational* areas involve your day-to-day responsibilities, such as answering the phone, filling out reports, and knowing how to coach and talk to your people. These are repetitive, reactive skills that you use daily.

- *Tactical* efforts help plan and manage actions to be taken in a year or less. Completing territory forecasts, planning how to arrange account assignments when someone is promoted or quits, filling out employee performance plans, and planning the multiple action steps necessary to close an important account are all tactical activities.

- *Strategic* efforts help you focus your team on the long run. Positioning your company's and sales force's selling philosophy and competitive message of uniqueness, planning or redefining your team's selling approach, and other activities that lead your salespeople and company toward a stronger selling focus or direction are all strategic endeavors.

These are all strategic management skills necessary to be a successful sales manager. Based on the time log you filled out in the last section, you should be able to evaluate how much time you normally spend on each of these operational, tactical, and strategic areas. If you are like most sales managers, you spend the majority of your time on operational issues, a minimum amount on tactical issues, and none at all on proactive strategic selling issues.

Most sales managers say there does not seem to be enough time during the week to focus on the proactive "big picture" strategic issues of their job; they are too busy fighting reactive operational fires all day. They also consistently lack time to spend dealing with tactical and strategic issues. Does this sound familiar? A successful manager needs to be more balanced in all the sales management skill areas.

Managers agree that managing the selling process and their salespeople are the two most critical responsibilities of sales management, but most still do nothing to change the way they spend their time. Are you controlling your job and responsibilities, or are they controlling you? If the answer is the latter, the solution is for you to decide to actually change the way you do your job.

The goal of all sales managers is to increase sales. Most managers and owners want their sales to increase, but they do not want to change their business or personal management styles. They are happy to force their salespeople to change; however, they simply do not want to have to change themselves.

Growing a business is like accelerating a car from 0 to 100 miles per hour. Most managers want an automatic transmission — as you apply more pressure to the gas pedal, the car magically speeds up until you release the pressure. In sales and sales management, however, you have a manual transmission. To successfully grow your team or business over the long run, you have to push in the clutch, reorganize your gear pattern, and increase your speed and acceleration at appropriate intervals.

The majority of businesses, especially small business, want to increase their sales and size, but they are unwilling to reorganize their structures to make this growth possible. Many of these businesses cannot grow much further in their current configurations. They must reorganize, reprioritize, and refocus their critical skills.

How are you evaluating and rearranging the skills you need for success as a sales manager? Shifting gears means getting rid of your accounts so you can spend 100 percent of your time managing your people and their selling efforts. It may also mean adding a new salesperson or reorganizing territory assignments. It means implementing the ideas we have already discussed and those presented in upcoming chapters.

If you are reading this book, it is safe to assume that you are already working at full speed. You have grown your responsibilities as a sales manager, but how much have you really changed your skills and emphasis to fit your management position? Ken Blanchard, coauthor of *The One-Minute Manager*, once said, "The things that get worked on first tend to get fixed first." What needs to be fixed in your business, and what have you been working on lately? If you have corporate political problems or are dealing with inventory shortages, you may not be investigating new strategies to boost your business.

The reality of sales management is that you have to really *want* to work on improving sales. You also either have to be willing to devote more time to sales management by doing less work in other areas or you need to delegate some of your responsibilities to free up your management time. Something has got to give if you are going to proactively improve your sales management skills. Remember, the only way you can significantly increase your business is by pushing in the clutch and reorganizing the way you do your job.

How interested are you in improving your salespeople and the focus of your selling efforts? The following steps can help you reorganize your job and develop your sales management skills:

1. Use your time log to evaluate how you are currently spending your time. What can you reorganize, delegate, or eliminate to balance managing your people and the selling process? What can you do to get rid of all the noncritical or reactive responsibilities you have picked up over the years?

2. Evaluate the tasks you are performing because you enjoy doing them as opposed to the tasks you need to be doing. Most businesspeople waste hours working on tasks they like even though other people could and should be doing them.

3. Evaluate how many of the small, detailed "stage-one" problems your people can handle on their own. These are the problems that fall in your lap or, worse, that you volunteer for because of your availability or easy access.

TEAM LEADER'S TOOL

MAKING TIME FOR STRATEGY

To balance your three management skill areas and free up time for more proactive, strategic management, you may need to employ the following tactics:

- Transfer your accounts to some of your salespeople so you can spend all your time managing your people and their selling efforts.
- Hire a new salesperson or reorganize existing territory assignments to relieve you of your personal territory assignments.
- Learn to say no to nonsales special projects that interfere with your sales management responsibilities.
- Learn to manage and/or reduce unnecessary paperwork for both you and your sales team.
- Shift from reacting to crises to helping your sales staff manage problems proactively.

SUMMARY

Being an effective sales manager requires you to shift the majority of your focus from reactive activities to proactive responsibilities. It obligates you to reduce the amount of time you spend on day-to-day operational tasks and increase the time you invest in long-term tactical and strategic efforts. To make this change, you need to reorganize and refocus your energy by eliminating job duties that hold you back and by concentrating on those duties that bring real results: motivating and managing your salespeople and the sales process. You may find it necessary to retrain some, or all of your sales people so they can take on these added responsibilities you now need them to be handling.

In the next chapter, we will look at different management styles and suggest ways to improve your own style.

EXHIBIT 2.1 THE FOUR STAGES OF EFFECTIVE CRISIS MANAGEMENT

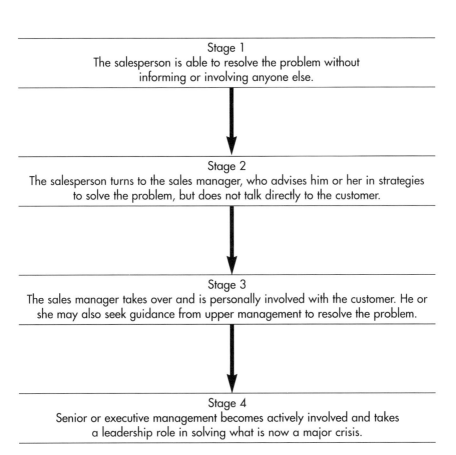

Stage 1
The salesperson is able to resolve the problem without informing or involving anyone else.

Stage 2
The salesperson turns to the sales manager, who advises him or her in strategies to solve the problem, but does not talk directly to the customer.

Stage 3
The sales manager takes over and is personally involved with the customer. He or she may also seek guidance from upper management to resolve the problem.

Stage 4
Senior or executive management becomes actively involved and takes a leadership role in solving what is now a major crisis.

EXHIBIT 2.2 SALES MANAGER'S TIME LOG

	Managing and Motivating Salespeople	Managing Selling Process	Selling Personal Accounts	Dealing with Administrivia	Practicing Crisis Management	Participating in Nonselling Projects
Monday			11:00–1:00 2:00–4:00	8:30–9:45 4:30–5:45	9:45–11:00 4:00–4:30	
Tuesday	10:00–11:00		3:00–4:30	11:00–1:30 2:30–3:00	4:30–5:15	8:30–10:00
Wednesday	1:00–1:30		1:30–3:00	8:30–10:00 11:30–12:15	3:00–3:45	10:00–11:30
Thursday			4:00–5:30	9:30–12:00 1:30–2:30	8:15–9:30 12:45–1:30	2:30–4:00
Friday		11:00–12:00	8:45–11:00	1:00–3:00		3:00–4:30

EXHIBIT 2.3 BREAKDOWN OF TIME SPENT ON PROACTIVE AND REACTIVE DUTIES

Activity	Real Time Spent	Goal Allocation for a Managing Manager
Selling personal customer accounts	_____%	_____%
Prospecting for new customers	_____%	_____%
Processing paperwork and internal bureaucracy	_____%	_____%
Intervening in crises and solving team problems	_____%	_____%
Handling nonsales-related projects	_____%	_____%
Motivating and managing your salespeople and their selling efforts	_____%	_____%
Helping your people with account strategies	_____%	_____%
Talking with your people to ensure their comfort and overall satisfaction with you and your company	_____%	_____%
Coaching your people on account problem resolution	_____%	_____%
Riding with your people to observe and coach their selling skills	_____%	_____%
Providing sales skill training and coaching	_____%	_____%

Chapter 3

Refining Your Management Style

In Chapter 2, we discussed how the successful sales manager needs to balance the two critical skills of managing the selling process and managing and motivating the sales force. The next chapter explains ways of building a motivational environment for your salespeople. Before you can build such an environment, however, you must examine the atmosphere you promote through your current managerial style. Although you need to concentrate on building your team's skills, it is crucial that you also continue to evaluate your personal management abilities, because the two are inherently linked. The majority of "motivational" problems experienced by salespeople are either caused or amplified by problems directly tied to the management skills of the owner or sales manager. This may seem like a fairly strong statement. How can a salesperson who continually causes problems at work or who does not do his or her job be a symptom of a management problem?

First, as a sales manager, you probably hired the "problem" person. If so, the real reason for that person's lack of motivation may be either your poor interviewing skills when you hired him or her or your poor firing skills at present. Sales managers often have significant problems with the first several salespeople they hire. It seems that only after gaining experience with several representatives who do not work out can they become more adept at hiring those who will. How long did the first salesperson you hired stay with you? What about the people you are hiring now? Chapter 6 details the hiring process and the steps in making effective choices.

The second way sales managers cause motivational problems is by failing to manage their people closely enough to create an environment that promotes success. Most people can sell successfully if they are properly trained and managed. Are you successfully coaching and training your people?

There are several ways to assess your effectiveness as a sales manager; one method is to evaluate your management style or philosophy. Although everyone is a blend of various management styles, we all have a bias toward how we approach managing others. What particular style best describes the way you manage your salespeople? What type of management style do your people recognize in you? What is it like to report to you on an ongoing basis?

There are four distinct types of sales managers: the drill sergeant, the administrivia manager, the top gun, and the coach. As we discuss each of these styles (the characteristics of which are highlighted in Exhibit 3.1), think about how you manage your salespeople. Evaluate how many of the positive and negative aspects of each style you tend to use with them. Also consider how your people would identify your particular form of sales management.

THE DRILL SERGEANT

Drill sergeant sales managers focus only on what a salesperson is doing wrong. This is the old "Theory X" style of management, which says that if you do not constantly watch your people, they will take complete advantage of you. The drill sergeant believes that all salespeople want to do as little as possible and that they will take complete advantage of any sign of management weakness they see. This type of sales manager thinks that people cannot be complimented for anything, reasoning that if you tell someone he or she is doing a good job, that person will immediately ask for a raise. When a salesperson has a great month in July, the drill sergeant asks, "But what have you done for me in August?"

These managers make statements like, "I don't care if my people dislike me, but they *will* respect me and work hard." They like the idea of being separate from the sales team. If sales representatives are a little afraid of their manager, so much the better. Drill sergeants believe people work harder with fear as a motivator. They also think that being friendly with salespeople makes managers vulnerable. They may say, "If you become too close to your people, your personal feelings may get in the way when you have to discipline someone."

This type of manager believes that good, hard-working salespeople are difficult to find because he or she does not trust the sales staff, assuming the worst whenever there is a problem. For example, if a customer calls and complains that a salesperson did not do what was promised, the drill sergeant immediately assumes the customer is right and the salesperson made a mistake. When the manager confronts the salesperson, he or she will immediately put that person on the defensive by the way the problem is presented.

According to the drill sergeant mentality, the only way to get an acceptable level of work out of anyone is to yell, scream, and constantly check up on them. Call reports are used as a reactive disciplinary mechanism instead of a proactive sales tool. The manager keeps a tight rein on team members' time, commenting on anyone he or she sees "standing around" during the day. Each minute people are not working is a minute they have taken advantage of their company and their manager.

Does this sound like any sales managers you know? All organizations need discipline and structure, and drill sergeants can provide this admirably. This style of management becomes negative only when it is the predominant style. As we said earlier, it is important to incorporate traits from each of the styles discussed here. You will have little impact if you have no disciplinary abilities; there are times when, as a manager, you need to give an order and know it will be followed. However, if people snap to attention when you enter a room, you may need to soften your drill sergeant style. Two ways to do this are to improve your positive communications with your people and to admit your mistakes.

Improving Communications

First, you need to honestly assess your positive and negative communications with your salespeople. Use the following questions as a starting point:

- Are the majority of your communications with your people positive or negative?
- When was the last time you complimented or gave positive feedback to one of your people?

- Are you checking on your sales staff to see if they are doing something right or doing something wrong?
- How do you approach your salespeople about customer complaints or problems?

Increasing positive communications and working to find people doing something right does not mean you have to become artificially sweet or plastic. It does mean working on improving your balance of positive and negative feedback.

Dr. Spencer Johnson, co-author of *The One-Minute Mother* and *The One-Minute Father*, presents the concept that children are unable to differentiate themselves from their actions. If a young child spills a glass of milk and is told how bad he or she is for making a mess, the child's self-esteem or self worth is weakened. This concept is relevant for managers because most adults cannot separate themselves from their actions either.

Watch how salespeople act if they lose a big sale or fall short of their quota for the year. They will either be depressed and make self-effacing personal comments about themselves, or they will try to sidestep responsibility by blaming their lack of performance on their manager, their company, their territory — anything except their own behavior. Either way, they will take your comments personally, causing them to spend more time repairing their self-esteem than fixing the real problem. It is important for people to accept and deal with the consequences of their actions. How can you give feedback or criticism in such a way that you help them keep their self-esteem and still deal with the short-term problem?

One way is to blend your comments, making positive statements about the person while interspersing comments about areas where he or she still needs improvement. Imagine that Kate, one of your salespeople, made a serious mistake on an order and your company lost a sale because of it. How would you handle the discussion? A drill sergeant manager would yell until he or she let off steam, focusing on his or her frustration and Kate's incompetence. The communication would be completely negative with a harsh delivery. A better way to handle the problem would be to confront Kate in the following way:

I know you're trying hard, but because you mishandled this account, our company has lost thousands of dollars. I know you feel badly about this, but you have caused a big problem. If it happens again, we'll have to take disciplinary action. You're normally conscientious and thorough, but I'm really angry that you let this whole situation get so out of hand. Now, you're a good sales rep and I don't want to lose you, so the next time this type of problem comes up, this is how I want you to handle it. …

By using this balanced approach, you can still say exactly how you feel and fully describe how angry you are, but the positive comments about the individual can help you increase the intensity and straightforwardness of your negative comments.

Admitting Your Mistakes

A major error drill sergeant managers make is to believe that they lose power and respect if their people see them make any type of mistake. When they do make an error, they try to cover it up so as not to "lose face." If you follow this course of action, you are teaching your salespeople that they should hide from or sidestep problems, which usually makes a problem worse.

By admitting your errors, you show that *you are not your actions.* Just because you made a mistake does not make you a "bad person." The essential thing is to correct the problem as honestly as possible. It is important for your people to know that you see yourself as human and are comfortable enough with yourself to admit that you have made a mistake or a bad decision. When this occurs, it is enough for you to say that the mistake has occurred so that it can be corrected as soon and as simply as possible. By presenting the situation as a problem to be solved, your people can learn by example to make suggestions for fixing the problem.

The Administrivia Manager

The administrivia manager is most interested in the details of selling. The neatness and completeness of a salesperson's call reports are more important to him or her than what that person actually did during the week. This type of sales manager believes that if you manage the details, the big things will fall into place. The administrivia manager is so focused on the minutia of the job that he or she never sees the big picture.

Remember that an important aspect of the sales manager's job is to give each salesperson an awareness of and insight into the tactical and strategic facets of selling. Administrivia sales managers are so concerned with paperwork that they tend to ignore their people. They spend the majority of the day behind their desks or in meetings, rarely talking with their salespeople. When they do talk to their representatives, they spend most of their time discussing paperwork, reports, and minor details of the job. They will put more emphasis on the accuracy and completeness of a sales forecast than on what the forecast really says.

New sales managers and managers who have never been salespeople tend to adopt this style of sales management. The job of managing salespeople is new or foreign to them, and they have no experience or training so they do not know what to focus on. By accomplishing something (anything) they can quantify and measure, they feel they can justify themselves to their managers. To their credit, they have the advantage of being organized and are usually well connected with other departments and managers.

Administrivia managers work long hours and try hard, but they focus on the wrong goals. Detail and report accuracy are important to any sales force, but they must be balanced with attention to the primary concerns of managing salespeople and the selling process. How much time do you spend on paperwork each week? Compare this to the amount of time you devote to managing and motivating your people and assisting with important account strategies.

Consider keeping a diary, like the one shown in Exhibit 3.2, that breaks down all the activities you are involved in during the day. List every activity, including talking on the telephone, attending meetings, talking to customers and salespeople, and so on. Divide the diary into 15-minute increments, and carry a timer or alarm with you to remind you to enter your activities promptly. This ensures the accuracy of your tracking, because if you wait to record several hours at once, you will most likely list what you *think* you did instead of what you *really* did. Keep your diary for a week, and you will have a fairly accurate summary of how and where you focus your energies. If you spend more time on paperwork than you do with your salespeople and customers, you are probably an administrivia manager.

Prism Management

It takes strict self-discipline to increase your tactical and strategic views of your job responsibilities and the people you manage. One way to overcome the reactive operational view is to embrace a proactive "prism" management style. This style lets you solve any problem with three simple solution alternatives.

A prism takes a single beam of light and refracts (divides) it into the different colors of the spectrum. A management prism allows you to take a problem and divide your solutions into operational, tactical, and strategic options. This process is illustrated in Exhibit 3.3.

Operational Option. The operational option tends to be the simplest and most widely used. The question here is, "What will solve this problem now?" An operational solution takes any problem at face value and can be used for a simple problem that requires a quick, easy answer.

Tactical Option. All problems are not as simple as those that can be solved using the operational approach. From the tactical point of view, we would ask, "What is the real problem here?" Many operational problems are only symptoms of larger, more complex problems, and if you only cure the symptoms, the problem never actually goes away. It keeps reappearing and growing, even though the symptoms may change. By applying a tactical approach, you may be able to solve the underlying problem once and for all.

Strategic Option. The third option, the strategic approach, asks, "What is the real situation we are dealing with?" It examines not only the problem itself, but the overall circumstances surrounding it. For example, suppose one of your salespeople comes to you and says that the Patterson account is demanding an additional 5-percent discount to close the sale. Your salesperson tells you the customer is buying only on price, and the sale will be lost without an immediate price break. How would you handle this situation?

If you take the operational approach ("What is the problem now?"), the answer is easy: Drop your price to get the business. If you use the tactical option ("What is the real problem here?"), the problem may be more complex. Perhaps the salesperson has never communicated your company's uniqueness or neglected to learn what the customer really wanted or who the competition was until it was too late to do anything about it. If any of these tactical issues are the real problem, a price cut will only solve a symptom. You will have to deal with this situation over and over. If you ask the strategic question ("What is the real situation we are dealing with?"), your answer may be that the customer has never accepted your uniqueness in the market and may not be a good fit for your company. Only a significant price cut could make you look competitive. If this is the case, cutting your price to get the business may lead to a major crisis in the future as you consistently try to satisfy a customer who demands service and support you cannot deliver.

What can you do to begin developing a more even balance between your strategic, tactical, and operational sales management efforts? Using the three prism management questions can increase your problem-solving flexibility and management success. Administrivia managers are overly reactive; they allow their salespeople and their selling environment to control them. They spend all of their time trying to apply operational solutions to problems that require more complex methods, so territory problems continue to build instead of being successfully resolved once and for all.

Reducing Paperwork

Another way to balance your administrivia tendencies is to decide how much time you need to spend each week on the tactical and strategic aspects of your job. By giving these aspects top priority, you may need to cut back on the operational administrivia demands (paperwork, internal meetings, and so forth) that most sales managers put first. When you look at your next paperwork request, consider the following questions:

- How many problems will be created if I skip this report?
- Is this report an essential, need-to-know request or an informational,

nice-to-know request?

- Can I delegate this report to someone who has more time?
- Will completing this report help me and my salespeople increase our selling success?

As a strategic sales manager, you need to protect yourself and your sales staff from others who want to collect information that will take time away from selling without contributing to your overall selling goals. An important part of your job is running interference and proactively challenging any meaningless internal information requests.

To ensure that operational paperwork does not consume your entire year, schedule strategy days with your people. Remember to discuss only big picture topics such as account strategies or territory planning. Some sales managers find they need to hold this type of meeting off-site to avoid being distracted by paperwork, details, and internal phone calls.

The reality of management is that administrivia will always fill in any time that is not specifically reserved for proactively managing your people and their selling efforts. How are you fighting the administrivia of your company?

The Top Gun

Top gun sales managers jump in and take over a sales call whenever possible. They believe their skills as the "best salesperson in the company" are more important than their management skills. Some people call this the "Lone Ranger" style of management because these sales managers want to rush in and save any call they feel is in distress, even when their help is not needed, wanted, or appreciated. Such managers believe they are the best and most qualified salespeople in their companies, and because of this, it is acceptable (even positive) to help sell any situation that does not seem to be going perfectly. They will even take over a sales call that is proceeding smoothly if they feel their approach or style of selling will close the business. A top gun manager sees the time he or she spends riding with salespeople as selling time, getting in the car each morning and saying, "Okay, let's go out and close some business today."

A lot of newer managers tend to subscribe to the top gun management style because, like new administrivia managers, they are not comfortable with being full-time managing managers. They think their personal selling skills were the reason for their promotion to sales manager — the company's way of reaffirming their personal ability to sell. This line of thinking leads to the belief that all their salespeople should sell the same way they do. As we discussed in Chapter 1, your selling ability is a "doing skill" that you need to give up as a sales manager. Most top gun sales managers are still learning how to manage others and to accept that their personal success is now based on others' efforts.

If you often behave as a top gun sales manager, step back and ask yourself the following questions the next time you feel the need to jump in and take over a sales call from one of your salespeople:

- Is this call really in trouble, or is the salesperson simply handling the sale differently than I would?
- Is it progressing slower or faster than I like?
- Does the customer seem as concerned as I do?
- What kind of problem will I cause if I interfere too early and take over a call he or she thought was going well?
- How will the customer react if I jump in and take over the selling effort?

Compare training your sales force to teaching a child to swim. Children swallow a lot of water when they are first learning to swim. Most parents are poor swimming instructors because they pull their child up the first time he or she swallows even a small amount of water. As loving parents, they make sure the child swallows as little water as possible, so they step in and help at the first sign of trouble. A professional instructor, on the other hand, will support and help the child, but only after he or she has swallowed a bit more water. Learning to swim successfully is based more on personal confidence and trust in your ability in the water than it is on any specific type of stroke or kick. In short, if the child never swallows any water, he or she will never learn to swim.

This a lot like teaching someone to sell. Salespeople will never be able to sell on their own until they are given the opportunity to fail on their

own. The difference between an amateur sales manager and a professional one is knowing how much "water" to let a newer person swallow before
jumping in to help. An experienced manager will let a salesperson strug-
gle for a while, realizing that if he or she steps in too soon, the salesperson
might not even realize that the call was in trouble. Letting a salesperson
experience some difficulty on a sales call will help them understand and
appreciate your eventual involvement.

As we stated earlier, a sales manager's job is to train and build a sales
team, not to do all the selling work. Top gun sales managers have a great
deal of expertise to draw on to help and train their salespeople, but they
focus on the professional details of closing the sale and ignore the need for
more tactical sales training and personal development. To help balance
your top gun characteristics, refer back to the time log you filled out in
Chapter 2 to assess how much time you are spending as a salesperson and
how much time you devote to managing salespeople. How much of your
day is taken up by doing rather than managing? One of the toughest points
for sales managers to learn is that salespeople learn by doing something
themselves, not by passively watching their managers do it.

THE COACH

The key to sales management in the next decade will be based on sales
managers' ability to coach and counsel their people. As we discussed in
Chapter 2, if you are going to grow your business and sales volume over
the next several years, you should be more involved with your salespeople
on a regular basis. The most positive way to do this is by being their coach.

Coaches realize that their goal is not to do the salesperson's job, but to
lead, guide, and train salespeople. This is their main focus. There are several critical components to being a successful coach, most of which we
have already mentioned:

- Ensure that the majority of your communications are positive.
- Try to find your people doing things correctly and compliment them
  on these things, instead of just looking for mistakes and negative
  aspects of their performance.

- Make sure that when you address negative activities, you also affirm the salesperson's positive qualities.
- Be proactive in the selling process by getting involved with each of your people to help them with strategies for their selling territories.

EVALUATING YOUR SALES MANAGEMENT STYLE

A successful sales manager blends all four of the management styles described into a balanced whole. If you are unsure of your managerial blend, consider asking your salespeople to isolate your strongest skills and to identify areas you could enhance that would help them be more successful in their jobs. You may want to list the four management styles we have discussed and ask the team to classify you based on the characteristics listed. You may find it easiest to distribute a form, such as the one shown on pages 217–218 of Appendix A, and ask that it be completed and returned to you anonymously.

Another alternative is to ask a sales manager you respect how he or she would classify your management style and what areas he or she thinks you could improve.

The goal is to get feedback. Information is power, and the more you know about your own style of sales management, the stronger and more successful you will be as a leader.

SUMMARY

An important step in enhancing your management skills is to evaluate your management style or philosophy. The four basic types of sales managers we have discussed in this chapter — drill sergeant, administrivia, top gun, and coach — all have positive and negative aspects. Once you identify your dominant style, you can work on balancing and blending all four to create a style that can be used to successfully train and manage your sales team.

In Chapter 4, we discuss the role self-esteem plays in your management style and how you can build your own self-esteem to become a more effective sales manager.

EXHIBIT 3.1 CHARACTERISTICS OF THE FOUR SALES MANAGEMENT STYLES

Drill Sergeant
- Does not really trust people
- Focuses only on what salespeople are doing wrong
- Believes salespeople want to do as little as possible
- Perceives any compliments and encouragement as management "weaknesses" that a sales staff will try to take advantage of
- Remains aloof from salespeople, associating friendliness with vulnerability
- Relies on yelling and screaming as a primary management and motivational tool

Administrivia
- Has a strong operational focus
- Values neatness and completeness over activities or accomplishments
- Focuses on minutia and loses sight of the big picture
- Ignores salespeople; spends little time communicating with them
- Focuses on the detailed, quantifiable parts of the job to justify his or her existence to upper management

Top Gun
- Feels his or her selling skills were the only reason for his or her promotion to sales manager
- Jumps in and takes over a sales call even when help is not wanted, needed, or appreciated
- Focuses on personally closing sales, overlooking the need for sales training and personal development of the sales force
- Expects all salespeople to sell exactly the way he or she does

Coach
- Is involved with salespeople regularly and consistently
- Works proactively with all salespeople
- Leads, guides, and trains people in a positive way
- Makes the majority of his or her communications positive; catches people doing things right and tells them so
- Coaches people through strategies and plans for their territories and accounts
- Does not condone incompetence, but tries to teach and guide behavioral change in a positive way

EXHIBIT 3.2 DETAILED DIARY FOR SALES MANAGERS

Time	Activity
8:00	Review monthly sales forecasts
8:15	" " "
8:30	Phone calls to personal accounts (Acme Printing, Repro Art)
8:45	" " "
9:00	Weekly sales managers' meeting
9:15	" " "
9:30	" " "
9:45	" " "
10:00	" " "
10:15	" " "
10:30	" " "
10:45	" " "
11:00	Return phone messages
11:15	" " "
11:30	Discuss problem client w/ Bob
11:45	" " "
12:00	Lunch with sales rep (Anne) and client
12:15	(Baxter Jones—Very Bright Printers)
12:30	" " "
12:45	" " "
1:00	" " "
1:15	" " "
1:30	Return phone messages
1:45	" " "
2:00	Prepare performance appraisal for Gina
2:15	" " "
2:30	" " "
2:45	" " "
3:00	Review and approve expense reports
3:15	" " "

3:30	Work on next year's budget
3:45	Help Max with scheduling problem
4:00	Phone call from Acme Printing
4:15	Work on next year's budget
4:30	" " "
4:45	" " "
5:00	Make up invitations for company picnic and photocopy
5:15	" " "
5:30	" " "
5:45	" " "
6:00	

EXHIBIT 3.3 PRISM MANAGEMENT STYLE

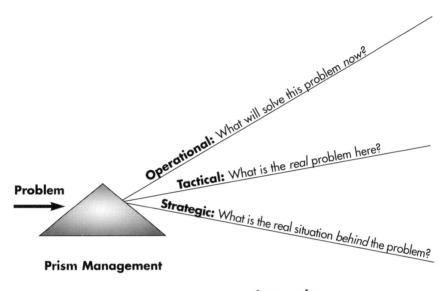

Problem

Prism Management

Approaches

Operational: What will solve this problem now?

Tactical: What is the real problem here?

Strategic: What is the real situation behind the problem?

CHAPTER 4

THE ROLE OF SELF-ESTEEM IN SUCCESSFUL SALES MANAGEMENT

Bill McGrane III, a self-esteem expert from Cincinnati, defined self-esteem as the respect a person feels for himself or herself. Having self-esteem means you do not have to measure yourself or your achievements against others and that you do not have to use comparative language, such as "I'm better than he is," or "She's smarter than I am." This does not mean you need to accept your current situation. You can have self-esteem and still continue to work hard to improve. The higher your self-esteem, the more comfortable you will be with who you are today, even as you work toward what you want to be tomorrow.

ELEMENTS OF SELF-ESTEEM

Take a moment to complete the self-esteem evaluation form shown in Exhibit 4.1. How do you feel about yourself? How content are you with who you really are? When you look in the mirror, how comfortable are you with what you see? Do you accept your looks, personality, relationships, and professional achievements? How do you feel about watching others in your company succeed? People with low self-esteem have an urgent need to always win no matter what. They feel that if someone else wins, even in an area that does not affect them, it means they lose, and losing means they are less as a person.

In Chapter 1, we talked about whether you are a doer, a doing manager, or a managing manager. Your level of self-esteem can either help or hinder your ability to become an effective managing manager. Is your self-esteem based on who you are or on what you do? Think about it. How important is your job title to you? If you only define yourself by your actions or accomplishments ("I'm important because I'm a sales manager"), your self-esteem can be severely reduced if something jeopardizes your job. Almost half of all sales managers eventually return (by choice) to full-time selling at some point in their careers. If you link your self-esteem to being a sales manager, how would you feel about going back to a full-time selling position? You would not have changed as a person, but would you feel the same about yourself?

How do you define yourself? People with low self-esteem tend to define themselves based on what they do or have accomplished. They have a strong need to make sure that everyone knows exactly how successful they are. We have all met these people — they put great effort into impressing others with their achievements.

The issue of self-esteem is one of the major issues most sales managers face in making the transition to managing manager. If you only define yourself based on what you have done rather than on who you are, maintaining a personal list of accounts will be critical to your personal definition of success. Your personal selling efforts become a safety net if you perceive your sales management skills as being less than perfect. This is the doing manager mentality; even if your people did not make their numbers for the year, at least you can claim that you made your own sales quota. Do you feel uncomfortable releasing your doing activities and moving to a full management position because it will take away from how you see yourself?

If this is an issue for you, consider finding a mentor to help you become more comfortable with your changing role as a manager and as a person. Search out a more experienced managing manager, and ask how he or she dealt with this difficult transition.

How you feel about yourself is the most critical foundation of your ability to manage and motivate others. Bill McGrane teaches people to build their self-esteem daily by looking in the mirror and using affirmations such as, "I now accept myself totally and unconditionally." You also need to evaluate what you say to others. How negative and/or positive are your communications? The more positive your interactions and attitude, the more comfortable and secure you will be with yourself.

TEAM LEADER'S TOOL

INCREASING YOUR SELF-ESTEEM

If your answers to the self-evaluation form show that your self-esteem needs to be strengthened, consider taking these steps:

- Find an experienced managing manager to serve as your mentor. To help you feel more comfortable with your changing role, ask how that person made the transition from doing manager to managing manager.
- Try repeating affirmations that can build your self-esteem. Look in the mirror every day and repeat statements like the following:
  "I now accept myself totally and unconditionally."
  "I now free myself from all self-destructive criticism."
  "I now choose to be completely self-determined and allow others the same right."
  "I now release all comparisons between myself and others."
- Watch your words. Keeping your communications with others positive and affirming can help you and others feel more comfortable and secure.

SELF-ESTEEM AND MANAGEMENT STYLE

Once you have worked through how you feel about yourself, the next step is to look at how you manage others. What is it like to work for you? How much of your management style is based on affirming and supporting individuals rather than pressuring people for results?

Self-esteem is a lifelong process of working on a daily basis to feel better and more accepting of who you are. This, in turn, makes it easier for you to accept others as they are. The more self-esteem you have as a sales manager, the more capable you will be of managing and motivating your salespeople. As a manager, success with your salespeople is based on (1) personal management style and (2) the atmosphere you create for your sales force. (Exhibit 4.2 compares the characteristics of managers with low self-esteem to those with high self-esteem.)

As a sales manager with high self-esteem, you are comfortable working to make your people feel affirmed and important. Although you still have required standards of performance, you are accepting and supportive of the people reporting to you. You know that people work hardest and achieve the most when they feel good about themselves and their environment.

A sales manager with low self-esteem thinks people work hardest and achieve the most when they are uncomfortable or scared. He or she wants to be the star of the department and receive all the recognition because of his or her exceptional leadership skills. The higher your self-esteem, the more attention you focus on your people. Allowing your team to have the spotlight creates an environment that makes them want to work harder.

For example, Joan worked as a salesperson for a large manufacturer and closed a big sale. Competition was fierce, and she won the order over most of her major rivals. The owner of the company offered his congratulations to Bill, the sales manager, on closing the sale. Bill said he was glad the owner was pleased and that everyone on his team had worked hard to win the account. He added that Joan was the real force behind the achievement. "It would mean a lot," Bill said, "if you told her personally how impressed you are with the job she did." A sales manager who lacked self-esteem would probably have said, "Thanks for the feedback," when the owner expressed pleasure over the new account. But a manager who is comfortable in his or her position wants the salesperson to receive recognition and affirming feedback from senior management.

The happier you are with yourself, the more energy and effort you can direct toward others. There is a "chain of success," illustrated in Exhibit 4.3, that forms when a sales manager has a high level of self-esteem. When you are comfortable enough to give your salespeople more attention and recognition, they tend to work harder. The harder they work, the more they produce; the more they produce, the greater the chances are you will achieve your own objectives. Are you successful because of your great leadership skills? Or are you successful because of your ability to bring out the best in the people who report to you?

In previous chapters, we used various methods to identify and assess your personal management style. As you have probably noticed, the areas tend to overlap. The management style characteristics you identified in Chapter 3 are probably consistent with your level of personal and professional self-esteem. To complete the assessment of your personal management style, you should to evaluate your skills in three important areas:

1. *Your view of your salespeople* — do you feel they *work* for you or *report* to you?
2. *The source of your power as a sales manager* — how much of your effectiveness is derived from "position power" versus "personal power"?
3. *The balance of your communications with others* — how much of your communications as a sales manager is negative? how much is positive?

Your View of Your Salespeople

As a manager or owner, do you feel your salespeople work for you, or do they just report to you? The difference is significant. When you encourage people to *report* to you, it is a sign of your high self-esteem. A reporting philosophy identifies and affirms your respect for each individual.

Feeling that your people *work* for you can signal a negative or low self-esteem style of management. Managers who feel their salespeople work for them usually like to be called "boss." They enjoy feeling that they are the benevolent rulers of their kingdoms. This type of manager enjoys an authoritarian management style, gaining a sensation of strength and power as a manager by having people view him or her as an authority and a superior. Although respect for authority and the structures of your company are important for any employee, you do not want people to think they need your permission before they make even the smallest move.

Another way to view this situation is to consider how you want your salespeople to feel about their job and their relationship with you. How open do you want discussions and feedback to be? Do you want your people to be comfortable telling you when they disagree or feel there is a better way to do something? How much initiative do you want them to use in their jobs?

For example, Don, a sales manager, was a terror to work with. His comments to his salespeople were consistently negative; no one's performance was ever good enough; he expressed his anger loudly by yelling at his people and pointing out their mistakes during sales meetings; and he openly made fun of the lower performers on the team. Several members of his sales force complained of being afraid to take customer problems to him because he would angrily blame them for not handling their problems alone. Because of this fear factor, salespeople delayed in taking their problems to Don until they had become real crises, and, by that time, were almost impossible to solve. In this harsh environment, salespeople also stopped bringing up ideas or making suggestions. Their negative attitude spread through the company as well as to Don, who would have looked good if their ideas had succeeded.

How do you treat a salesperson who seeks your help in solving a customer problem? How many suggestions or new ideas have you received from your salespeople in the last two weeks? It is important that your people understand and respect your final decision-making responsibility, but you can attain respect for your authority as a manager and still maintain an empowered environment in which you encourage people to work *with* you rather than *for* you. (We discuss empowering employees in Chapter 5.)

Your Source of Power

There are two types of power anyone can have within an organization: position power and personal power. *Position power* is derived from the inherent respect people in a company have for a particular job title or assignment. Workers may personally dislike a company president, but because of his or her position, that person will still be accorded respect and authority by the staff. How much of your success as a sales manager is based on your position power? Position power has been proven to be a poor motivator within a sales force. Very few people respect someone because they have to.

The second, more effective, type of power is personal power. *Personal power* is your ability to lead and motivate your people because they like you and want to follow you. Strong personal power gives you a definite leadership ability no matter what your title or job description.

In our earlier example, Don, the sales manager, had strong position power but almost no personal power. He got respect and action because of his position, but he was actually missing out on new ideas because of his lack of personal power with his team.

Sales managers who feel they do not have enough personal power and who consistently exert their control through position power are those who want to be seen as being above their salespeople. "I'm your sales manager because I'm better and know more about selling," is a common statement from this type of manager. Managing by position power means you tend to give drill sergeant-type orders to your salespeople instead of asking or coaching them through discussion. A position power sales manager tells his or her people exactly what he or she wants done. Orders are given in a "no-questions-allowed" style of communication. This manager knows just what he or she wants and tells everyone what they are to do. Other people's suggestions and opinions are not encouraged because a position power manager never likes to look bad or be corrected.

A personal power sales manager goes to the sales team and asks for their opinions. He or she may eventually give an order for final action to be taken, but only after his or her people have been given a chance to comment. Personal power managers accept that they will occasionally make mistakes. They are always receptive to other opinions. This does not mean the manager will agree, but he or she feels it is important that salespeople know they can always discuss or question the actions to be taken.

A position power bias means you only manage results. "Yes or no, did you close that account today as I told you to do?" is a strong position power statement.

Notice how all this ties into the issue of self-esteem. A sales manager with high self-esteem has such a high level of personal power that position power becomes secondary. A sales manager with low self-esteem continually "pulls rank" on people and feels the need to constantly remind them of who is in charge. Low self-esteem managers must always throw their title and position around to achieve their goals.

Reliance on position power also affects the way you view mistakes.

How comfortable are you identifying your mistakes to others? Sales managers who depend heavily on position power are concerned about always having the right answer. They believe they risk a significant loss of power and impact if they are ever seen as being wrong. Do you admit to mistakes or bad decisions so they can be corrected as soon and as simply as possible? As we discussed in Chapter 3, it is important for you to be able to say, "I'm sorry, that was wrong. Let's fix it and do it this way instead."

Your Communication Style

Several years ago, *The Wall Street Journal* highlighted a study showing that 90 percent of all communication between managers and employees was negative. What is the ratio of your positive to negative communications? During your next sales meeting, quietly ask one of your people to keep track of how many negative, positive, and neutral statements you make during the meeting. Keep your tracking confidential until after the meeting so meeting participants will not be biased. You may also ask your people to rate you. Have them write down the percentage of negative and positive comments they receive from you. To keep the feedback honest, insist that the rating be done anonymously.

What percentage of what you say is negative? In your sales meetings, how much of the information covered is of a positive nature? When was the last time you told any of your people what a good job they were doing? When did you last go out of your way to show how impressed you were with the way they handled a specific account situation?

Here is one example of why positive comments are so important. A large bank's goal was to move itself into a stronger selling culture. Most of its efforts were directed toward helping its salespeople (called loan officers) to initiate new business instead of waiting for customers to call. One of the loan officers' most significant complaints was the treatment they received from the bank's corporate loan committee. Commercial loan officers do not personally approve or reject loans. The central corporate loan committee reviews all official loan requests. A loan officer takes all loan applications, properly prepared and screened for credit, to this committee. In the resulting meeting, it is the loan officer's responsibility to present the loan application and try to "sell" it to the committee. The bank's front-line loan officers were frightened of the loan committee and did not like taking applications in for approval because the head of the committee always "grilled" them, asking such difficult, negative questions that even when a loan was approved, they felt like they had lost and looked bad to upper management.

To help this situation, consultants persuaded the credit executive to be a little more positive during the loan review meetings. This still did not resolve the problem, so each loan officer's manager was asked to sit in on the loan review meetings. After a meeting was over, the officer's manager sat down with him or her and reviewed what he or she did right as well as what they could have done better. There were still discussions about what the officers could do to enhance future presentations, but now the communications were balanced instead of concentrating on the negative. Because of this post-loan review coaching, the loan officers' attitudes eventually improved and they became more comfortable bringing loans to the committee.

How many meetings with your sales staff parallel the sessions of the bank's commercial loan committee? What can you do to make your meetings and communications more balanced instead of just focusing on negative feedback? Try the following suggestions:

- When you must give a salesperson negative feedback, talk to him or her alone in a private setting. Even when people agree with their manager's comments, they can be forced into defending themselves if they feel their friends or peers can hear the conversation.
- When you give feedback to anyone, make sure it is balanced. As we discussed in Chapter 3, many people have trouble separating their actions from their self-esteem. It is important to affirm positive aspects of the person while you identify how you want their negative behavior to be corrected.

Team Leader's Tool

Focusing on the Positive

Here are four steps you can take to make your communications more balanced and preserve or enhance your people's self-esteem.

1. Make a few positive statements about salespeople in every meeting. Be sincere and factual, and make the comments relevant to their jobs and sales performance.
2. Each time you talk with a salesperson, try to make some accurate and positive statement of how he or she is doing on an account.
3. Balance negative feedback with positive comments. Tell your people they are doing a good job. Identify what they have done well in a specific account situation, and then focus on what they can do to enhance performance rather than what they are doing wrong.
4. When you must give negative feedback, do so in private, not in front of the rest of the staff. Remember to separate the person from the action. Focus negative comments on the behavior, while making positive comments about the person.

Be aware that in a significant crisis, this positive/negative approach to feedback may not be appropriate. When you want someone to understand the severity of the situation, try giving all the negatives up front. When you are sure the representative understands how serious the error was, how much the error will cost, how difficult it will be to correct the problem, and how angry you are, then make some positive comments to reinforce your belief in the individual.

Summary

Managing and building an individual's self-esteem is the core of successful management. Your ability to manage and build others' self-esteem depends on how you feel about yourself. The more self-esteem you have as a manager, the more easily you can manage and create a climate in which people will be motivated. In Chapter 5, we look at more in-depth methods of creating a motivational environment.

Exhibit 4.1 Self-Esteem Evaluation Form

Personal Self-Esteem

- How content are you with yourself and who you really are?
- How accepting are you of your following characteristics?

  Weight _____

  Looks_____

  Personality _____

  Relationships _____

  Work achievements_____

  Financial strength _____

- Do you accept yourself as who you are or as what you do?
- How do you feel about yourself overall?

Managerial Self-Esteem

- How do you relate to and communicate with your people?
- How comfortable are you in watching and affirming the success of others in your company?
- What do you do to make sure your people are recognized for their accomplishments?
- How important is your title to you?
- What do you need to reevaluate or change to increase your success as a sales manager?

EXHIBIT 4.2 TRAITS OF MANAGERS WITH HIGH AND LOW SELF-ESTEEM

Low Self-Esteem
- Does not affirm people or make them feel important

- Has a strong need to take credit for what his or her people produced

- Believes that people work hardest and achieve most when they are uncomfortable or scared

- Defines self in terms of his or her actions and accomplishments; needs to let others know how successful he or she is

- Finds it difficult to base his or her success on the selling success of others; is often reluctant to release personal accounts and other "doing" activities that are critical to his or her definition of personal success

- Has an urgent need to win under any circumstances

High Self-Esteem
- Affirms people and makes them feel important, while still requiring them to meet certain minimum standards of performance

- Focuses lots of attention on people and gives credit to those who have done a good job

- Understands that people work hardest and achieve most when they accept and are comfortable with themselves and their environment

- Defines self in terms of who he or she is as a person

- Is comfortable basing his or her success on the selling success of others

EXHIBIT 4.3 THE SALES MANAGER'S CHAIN OF SUCCESS

CHAPTER 5

CREATING AN ATMOSPHERE FOR ACHIEVEMENT

In this chapter, we look at the motivational environment you are build-ing for your sales team. As we have already stated, your success with your people is based on your personal management style and on the motivational atmosphere you create. How are you helping your salespeo-ple enhance their skills to keep them growing and competitive in your changing marketplace?

THE FUNDAMENTAL ELEMENTS OF TRAINING

In evaluating how to train your sales staff, it is helpful to examine how zoo trainers work with large cats, such as Bengal tigers, mountain lions, and cheetahs, for public shows. How do you train wild animals that weigh more than you do and could easily kill you if they wanted? This situation paral-lels the environment many sales managers feel they work in on a daily basis.

Animal trainers have identified some fundamental philosophies that are critical to the safe and successful training of animals:

- It is important that the animal trust the trainer and that they learn mutual respect. The cat needs to see consistent behaviors and actions, so it knows what to expect from the trainer.
- The animal needs to know it is loved and admired. The trainers constant-ly touch and stroke the cats to make sure they are continually reaffirmed.
- Most important, training an animal is based on rewarding correct behavior. It takes years to train a cat to jump through a hoop. Trainers start with a line across the floor of a room. When the cat crosses the line, it is given positive recognition and a small food reward to focus its attention on the positive action. The most significant turning point in training comes when the cat realizes the reward is tied to its actions. Once the trainer gets the cat to cross the room on command, the rest is relatively easy. The markings on the floor are slowly replaced by a large hoop, which eventually becomes a smaller hoop touching the floor and then a hoop that is gradually raised in the air.

Look at the fundamentals of training wild animal experts used and compare them to child and adult training concepts. The concepts are identical even though the environment and implementation are radically different.

Take, for example, the process of training a person to increase his or her sales success. As the sales manager, you must show the person how much you respect and care about him or her as an individual, be consistent in your expectations and behavior, and prove that he or she has your support. You need to offer direct rewards for positive behavior by focusing on what the person does properly instead of dwelling on his or her mistakes. Successful training also requires you to make a significant investment in ongoing training. Even though the working environments are completely different, the basic tenets of behavior modification and successful training are the same in the sales arena as they are in a zoo.

How many of these ideas already exist in the environment you have built for your salespeople? What are you willing to change or improve to increase the success and motivation of each of your team's members?

One concept of team motivation holds that, beyond our most basic needs of food, shelter, and safety, we are moved by the need for love and acceptance. Why do salespeople rush back to the office after closing a big sale to tell their sales manager about their success? Why do so many salespeople fight so hard for attention and recognition from their managers and peers? Attention and recognition are variations of love and acceptance.

What is it like to work for you and your company? How much attention and recognition do your people receive? Even when you use a strong, "persuasive" management style, motivating a salesperson to increase his or her productivity is still one of the most difficult challenges any manager faces. Just making sure your people are recognized and appreciated will not get the job done in a highly competitive market. It is just not enough. So, how do you motivate a group of salespeople to achieve more for you and your company?

MOTIVATION BASICS

Self-esteem expert Bill McGrane identified four points of motivation:

1. You cannot motivate anyone to do anything. This is significant because most companies and managers spend significant amounts of time trying to get their sales teams motivated. The reason you cannot motivate people to do anything is given in point 2.

2. People are already highly motivated. If you are breathing, you are highly motivated. Many sales managers may start laughing at this point and begin to identify truly unmotivated salespeople who report to them. However, the problem is not that people lack motivation, it is that they all have different motivations.

3. People are motivated for their own reasons, not yours. Look at someone you think is unmotivated. He or she may be moved to action by reasons you cannot begin to know unless you examine his or her background and past experiences. Motivation can be affected by bias, self-esteem, culture, upbringing, or past treatment. The differences are varied, and not everyone's motivational focus will agree with yours.

   We all want to receive the maximum reward for the minimum effort. How many people do you know who want to work hard for the sheer joy of it? All business enhancements and innovations are based on the concept of less effort for greater results. This is referred to as "increased productivity" in business, but sales managers call it a lazy work ethic when it applies to their work force.

4. All you, as a sales manager, can do is create an environment for people to motivate themselves.

   What kind of motivational environment have you created for your people? The answers to the following questions can give you an accurate idea of your department's current standing in this area:

- How motivated are your people to get the job done even when you are not around?

- How much time and effort have you invested in rebuilding or strengthening the motivational environment of your business?

- How much feedback have you gotten from your people about their work environment?
- What kinds of rewards and recognition do you give for top performance? Who decided these were the best rewards to help enhance the motivational environment? Did you ask your people, or did you make the decision yourself based on your own experiences and preferences?

Your personal bias is one of the most significant problems you face as a sales manager. If you are not careful, the motivational environment you build will work for you rather than for your sales team. Look at your company's reward and bonus system. It probably excites the management team more than it does the sales force. Consider asking your people what most excites them about their job and making a sale. Discuss with your entire sales team each of your bonus and promotion activities to find out how they feel about the benefits of your programs. The only way you can build an environment in which people motivate themselves is to discover what they really want. The most effective motivational atmosphere begins with open, honest communication.

TEAM LEADER'S TOOL

LETTING YOUR PEOPLE CHOOSE THEIR OWN REWARDS

The most effective motivating environment begins with open, honest communication between the sales force and its managing manager. Use the following suggestions to find out what motivates your people and what they really want.

- Examine the rewards and bonus system you offer. Ask yourself if it was set up based on the management team's preferences or those of the sales force.
- Ask your people what excites them about their job and making a sale.
- Discuss each of your bonus and promotion activities with your people to get their true feelings about the program's benefits.
- Redesign your plan to include the rewards and recognition your sales team requests.

CONTRIBUTORS TO MOTIVATION

When people talk about how to build an effective motivational environment, money is always mentioned. How important is money as a motivator? Have you ever heard anyone say, "If you really want to motivate a sales force, just pay them more?"

Of course, money does motivate people, especially salespeople. We discuss the details of effective sales pay plans in Chapter 11, but the bottom line of sales compensation is that you will attract and keep a higher-quality sales performer when you have a compensation system that pays more money for higher revenues. If you have a poorly designed pay plan, or if you are underpaying salespeople based on your competition, you will have a problem hiring and keeping the best salespeople.

Let us assume, however, that you have a competitive compensation package, and you pay your salespeople more money when they sell more. Will that keep them enthusiastic and motivated to work their hardest for the next several years? Probably not. A strong pay program is the foundation of an effective motivational environment, but it is only the beginning.

There are five major contributors that can help you maximize the motivational environment of your sales team (see Exhibit 5.1). You and your company do not need to have all five of these factors, but the more you have, the easier it will be to create an effective motivational atmosphere. If any of these points can never be present in your company, it simply means that you may need to overcompensate in the other four areas to enhance your environment. As we discuss each of the five motivators, evaluate where your company stands in each area and what you can do to strengthen your environment.

Advancement Opportunities

The first major contributor that can enhance your motivational environment is the type of advancement and career path open to each of your salespeople. What type of promotions can your people expect? If they do a good job and stay with your company for a long time, how and when will they be promoted to higher levels within your company? Most employees, especially salespeople, are motivated by the potential for advancement.

This factor allows your top performers to feel they are moving up and improving their position within their profession. Most salespeople are very promotion conscious and offering a career path with better job titles, more responsibility, and higher pay can have a significant effect on a salesperson's motivation.

Having different levels of job titles lets you identify your more experienced, high-volume achievers. For example, one large corporation calls all its salespeople "marketing representatives." Within this classification, there are several position titles. When you are hired by this corporation, you are called an "associate marketing representative." After at least three years of making annual sales quotas and proving you are a consistently high performer, you move up to "marketing representative." After at least five more years of strong performance and quota attainments, you may be promoted to "senior marketing representative." The most senior and experienced top performers are called "advisory marketing representatives." This latter group attends office management meetings and is actively involved in the interviewing and sales training process. The corporation pays on a salary-plus-commission basis, and salary ranges are defined by job titles, as are the amount of vacation given and other job "perks."

Do your people have advancement opportunities open to them? How can you increase or improve the job titles and career paths in your company?

Management Recognition

The second contributing factor to a strong motivational environment is management recognition. How does your company recognize your salespeople? Aside from job titles and positions, how do you give extra attention to your top performers? How do you make senior salespeople feel important to your company?

As we have already discussed, one of the best ways to recognize employees is through a career or promotion path within your company. If you are a larger corporation, you can lay out a 20-year career progression that involves better titles, better pay, and more responsibility. But what if you are a smaller company that has only 20 employees and three salespeople? Job titles are definitely not the way to offer stronger motivation: There is no corporate hierarchy for your salespeople to move up in. Even if you have only a few salespeople, there are still management efforts that can give them extra attention and support. One example is provided by a small office copier sales company that had four salespeople. To help enhance the motivational environment for the sales team, the owner made a point of going to lunch with every sales representative at least once a month to allow each of them some private, "one-on-one" time. He always used these lunches to have a mini performance review and to give each salesperson the opportunity to ask questions or bring up concerns or frustrations. The owner also made a point of telling each person how important he or she was to the company. He expressed personal appreciation for all their hard work and efforts. Although he lunched with each of the salespeople on a monthly basis, he met privately with his two senior representatives more frequently. He sought their leadership ideas as a way to show his recognition and appreciation of their greater sales contributions to his company. With such a small company, he did not have the luxury of several levels of job titles, but he was able to give his people some extra personal management time to help enhance their motivational environment.

Another way to increase management recognition is to give your senior representatives a little added flexibility or freedom in the way they do their jobs. Additional benefits need to be handled carefully. You want the differences offered to be great enough that people want to work for them, but not significant enough that you create two tiers of salespeople. A number of years ago, the airlines discovered the problems of treating their employees differently. The companies tried a two-tier pay structure for their pilots and cockpit crews to try to reduce labor costs. The pay and benefit differences were significant and created and "us versus them" environment. This environment became so disruptive to teamwork and motivation that the airlines were forced to return to the higher pay plan for all employees.

What can you do to offer your salespeople extra perks that are strong enough to help enhance their environment but not so extensive as to diminish teamwork? One manufacturing firm required its salespeople to travel extensively. The vice president of sales gave some small but important perks to her top sales performers. She had a policy that any salespeople who fulfilled at least 110 percent of their quota could fly first class on any of their business trips. The company cost of this offer was not that significant because most travel decisions were made at the last minute, and discounted fares were not usually available. But think about how salespeople felt when they were able to upgrade their seats at the company's expense. The vice president of sales also offered to pay any salesperson's annual membership for one of the airlines' private clubs if he or she had reached at least 100 percent of his or her quota the previous year.

In another instance, a small office supply company did quarterly inventory and restocking on a Saturday, and the salespeople were required to help with this task. As you would expect, it was not considered an exciting job, and the salespeople complained about it continually. Finally, Jim, the owner, announced that any salesperson who was at least 100 percent year-to-date with his or her quota would be exempt from the Saturday duty, and he would hire a temporary worker to take that salesperson's place. The impact of this offer was amazing. Exemption from Saturday work was more motivating than any of the other sales contests Jim had offered in the past.

What can you do to increase your management recognition and attention for your team? You might ask one of your top salespeople to accompany you to an association meeting or send them to represent your company at local chamber of commerce meetings or local civic activities. When was the last time you invited any of your senior salespeople to a management planning session? The goal is to offer ways to help your people feel important and affirmed.

Empowerment

The third major contributor that can enhance your motivational environment is increased responsibilities or challenges. Many companies call this *employee empowerment.* Empowering your people means proving your support by giving them the responsibility *and* the authority to complete a job successfully. This is not meant to take significant power away from the sales manager or owner, so salespeople may still not be in charge of major decisions. But if you give your people more authority and control over their job responsibilities, they can be moved to work harder for their own self-gratification.

How much control, responsibility, and authority do your salespeople have over their jobs? The more control people have over their jobs, the more likely they are to be motivated to achieve. They feel they own not only the job, but the results of their work. The management of one large computer corporation did not understand this concept. The salespeople were in charge of selling and installing hundreds of thousands of dollars worth of computer equipment. Yet they had to have a sales manager sign all requisitions for customer manuals. How would you feel if you were responsible for a million-dollar sales quota but could not approve a ten-dollar customer manual?

Look at the conflict most salespeople face. They are expected to make their numbers for the year, but they have almost no authority with which to do this. This situation also causes a great deal of conflict and difficulties for sales managers of many small companies. The owner hires you, as the manager, to lead the sales team. You are responsible for both the revenue goals and the successful performance of your sales team. You are given heavy responsibilities, but when you try to lead your team and make decisions, you find that the owner is not comfortable giving you the authority to make significant decisions without him. Does this sound familiar? Responsibility without authority can lead to significant frustration and demotivation.

Empowering your salespeople means giving them the authority to control at least some of their job responsibilities. One way to empower your salespeople may be to give them a little more flexibility on the pricing or services offered. For example, because a parts manufacturer's business had become increasingly competitive and price sensitive, the owner decided to allow her sales force to negotiate price, at least partially, without management preapproval. Instead of giving her people fixed prices and requiring all price concessions to be approved, she let the salespeople negotiate the price within a specified range. To make sure they did not automatically drop to the lowest price to make a sale, she also changed the commission structure so the commission dropped as the price dropped. Selling at list price meant the representative earned 100 percent of the available commission on that sale. Cutting the price 5 percent meant a 10-percent drop in commission, and a 10-percent price cut resulted in a 20-percent drop in commission. The owner expected her salespeople to be unhappy with the change, so she was surprised by their positive reaction. The team liked having more control over customer negotiations, and salespeople said they could close deals more quickly with the owner out of the decision loop.

Although this was a small change for this company, the additional combination of increased responsibility and authority significantly increased the sales team's morale and motivational environment. How can you empower your people more?

TEAM LEADER'S TOOL

EMPOWERING YOUR PEOPLE

Try these steps to empower your people:

1. Respond to their problems with a careful mixture of recommended strategy and positive feedback. Criticize the job activity, *not* the person. Say, *"Even if our drivers missed the delivery, it was still your responsibility to make sure this was delivered on time,"* not *"It was your responsibility, but because you don't seem to care anymore, it wasn't delivered on time."*
2. Ask what the person thinks should be done before you give orders.
3. When you use other people's suggestions, give them credit for their ideas.

Fair and Clearly Defined Goals

The fourth factor in our list of motivation-building tools is fair, clearly defined goals. Success is a phenomenal motivator, especially for salespeople. Do you assign your people sales quotas for the year? How clearly defined are your expectations?

Vague or constantly changing goals or quotas can have a significantly negative impact on any motivational environment. One computer software company was so disorganized, the sales force did not receive their annual sales quota assignments until May or June, five or six months into the year! How motivated would you be as a salesperson if you had no idea what your quota was for the first half of every sales year?

Perhaps the best example of undefined goals was a distribution company that sold products used in supermarket merchandising. The company published a series of extensive product catalogs that were mailed to its customers and prospects on a regular basis. It also had two separate sales departments: a reactive "order desk" sales force that took incoming catalog orders by telephone, and six full-time proactive telemarketers with assigned territories who called customers and prospects daily. The proactive group accounted for approximately 60 percent of all sales, and reactive catalog orders generated the remaining 40 percent. The "order desk" people were paid a salary plus a small bonus that was tied to sales; telemarketers were paid a salary plus commission.

Even though the company was highly dependent on the telemarketers' efforts, the owner made it clear that he did not recognize their importance. He believed that even without them, he would generate a level of sales from their territories. There was nothing wrong with this concept, except that he used it as a basis for assigning quotas and commissions. Each year, on a totally subjective basis, he set a specific sales goal for each territory. Every number was different, and the owner chose the numbers he felt could be generated with no input from the sales force. If he decided that a certain territory could generate $120,000 in sales without a salesperson's involvement, the company only paid commission on sales that surpassed that amount. The owner said he set these goals alone because he started the business and he knew better than anyone what each territory's potential was.

The company had two top sales performers, Bill and Vicki, who together generated higher sales revenues than the other four telemarketers combined. In a given year, the owner decided that Bill's and Vicki's territories could each generate about $200,000 without a salesperson, and he assigned them both $700,000 as an annual quota. Both representatives sold between $800,000 and $900,000 for the year, earning individual incomes of $100,000 in commissions and salary. Would you have been satisfied with their performance and incomes earned?

When the owner made up the following year's numbers, he decided that Bill's and Vicki's territories could really have generated $500,000 each, so no commission would be paid on the first $500,000 of sales in their territories. He also assigned each of them a $1 million quota for the year. The owner did not like paying either Bill or Vicki over $100,000, so he also capped the pay plan so that no salesperson could earn over $90,000 in any given year. As you have gathered by now, Bill and Vicki were both extremely motivated people. They were so motivated that they both left the company and formed their own organization in direct competition with their former boss, taking the majority of their customers with them.

What about you and your company? How fair and consistent are your procedures and pay programs? How many changes or cutbacks have been made to your pay plans or bonus programs over the past several years? Most salespeople expect to be challenged in their jobs and to be held responsible for boosting production and revenues each year. What can you do to make your sales environment even more fair and consistent?

You need to make sure that important verbal announcements are always followed up in writing and distributed to all staff so that messages are not misinterpreted. One company published an employee "Bill of Rights" that outlined exactly how disagreements and problems would be handled. By documenting these procedures, management ensured that all staff understood the process and could be assured of fair and consistent treatment. Another organization held annual goal-setting sessions with management and the entire sales force.

A Sense of Team Purpose

The fifth and final motivator is the team purpose concept. How are you, as a sales manager, working to ensure that each of your people is a positive contributing member of your sales team? One company begins every sales meeting with each person identifying two positive things — one personal and one sales related — that happened to them since the last meeting.

Developing an affirming work atmosphere where each of your salespeople feels he or she is part of a total team purpose is a major contributor to the motivational environment. Building a "team" selling concept instead of a "star" system of recognition is vital.

The Star Approach. As you might guess, the star system only focuses on top performers and is based on the ineffective management philosophy of past decades that we discussed in Chapter 1. The sales manager spends all his or her time and attention working with the best salespeople. The idea is that underachievers will either survive and grow into top performers or they will "get the message" and leave. The mindset is, "If my lower performers want my help and attention, they have to earn it."

One star sales manager named Joe managed seven sales representatives in a large publishing company's Northwest division. Two of the salespeople were experienced, three were good and improving with experience, and the other two were rookies. Joe constantly complained about being overworked and devoted the majority of his time to his two top performers and the major accounts they covered. His attitude was, "I don't have time to work with my beginners; I'm too busy trying to make sure my senior people make their numbers. I can only focus on the selected efforts that will help me and my team generate the most business so I can make my quotas." The only time he spent with the mid-level and junior salespeople was at monthly group sales meetings where he pushed everyone for orders. The junior representatives wasted a lot of time waiting for time with Joe because they did not realize he was ignoring them on purpose.

Faced with his unavailability, they put in a lot of hard work on projects without accomplishing very much. One of the mid-level representatives finally left the company in frustration.

By working only with top members of your team, you ignore a percentage of your salespeople and the opportunity they have to produce additional revenues. You also accept the reactive short-term view of working and worrying only about what you can close within the next two or three months. Many small business owners have this view, and their sales force development tends to follow a consistent cycle, illustrated in Exhibit 5.2.

Most owners put an advertisement in the local newspaper whenever they need a new salesperson. After minimal interviewing, they hire the first reasonably qualified candidate, making the selection based on "gut instincts" and rarely check references or past work experience. When the new salesperson reports for work, they provide minimum sales training that focuses only on the basics of their products and services. The new person is given a weak territory from which the best accounts have been pulled and given to the most senior sales representatives. Once the new person has begun working his or her territory, owners again focus all of their time on their senior salespeople with top accounts. Of course, the new representative sells little without training or guidance. He or she is fired after nine months or so because of low sales.

The Team Approach. A better, more effective way to work with your people is through the team management approach. As the manager of a team, your job is to manage and motivate all your team members. The goal of a sales manager is to help his or her people achieve more than they would on their own. Even with normal short-term quotas and performance pressures, you are still most likely to make your numbers when all of your people are working at their maximum potential.

Successful team managers balance their time so everyone gets some type of sales training, strategic coaching, and problem-solving assistance on a regular basis. As the leader of a sales team, it is critical that you effectively interview and hire people with the most potential within your salary ranges. You also need to organize a comprehensive sales training program to bring new employees up to speed as soon as possible. It is your ongoing responsibility to coach and grow each of your salespeople so they can maximize their full revenue potential to your company. It is a stretch to assume you can turn a $100,000 producer into a $900,000 producer in less than a year, but you can work with each of your people to get significant performance increases.

What percentage of your efforts have you focused on short-term, operational problem solving, crisis management, and paper shuffling? How much of your time is invested in strategic planning, skills training, and on-site sales coaching with each of your people? If you answer this by saying you just do not have the time, you need to realize that customer and competitive environments have changed. You need to change, rearrange, and reprioritize your management views as a sales manager if you and your company are to remain competitive in your market.

Of course, this is difficult. Every sales manager has time constraints, demanding quotas, a shortage of trained people, and delivery and product problems. The question is: How will you redefine your job as a sales manager to add a tactical and strategic approach to your environment? Even if you rearrange your schedule to free only one or two hours a week for tactical or strategic management efforts, you are taking positive action to improve the motivational environment for your salespeople.

When you approach your salespeople as a team rather than a star structure, you will enhance your competitive advantage and increase your total sales.

SUMMARY

The only way to motivate people and achieve and improve your sales goals is to help your team members create their own motivational environment. The five major factors of motivation can help you create an environment in which all of your people — not just your top performers — exceed expectations. Using a team approach, there are several areas in which you are responsible for managing and motivating your people. The first of these, effectively hiring new salespeople, is discussed in the next chapter.

EXHIBIT 5.1 CONTRIBUTORS TO MOTIVATION

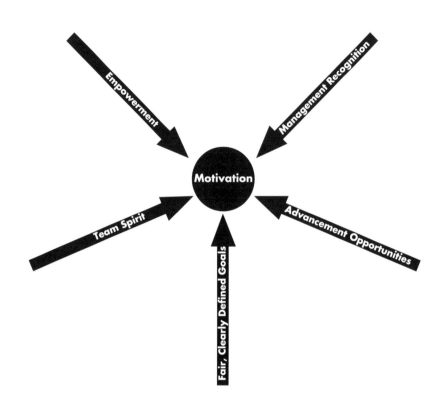

EXHIBIT 5.2 STAR SYSTEM TURNOVER CYCLE

PART II

MANAGING THE SELLING PROCESS

From an emphasis on the motivational environment and your personal managerial style, we move to a focus on the second major responsibility of the sales manager: managing the selling process. Although the topics in both parts are interdependent, Chapters 6 through 11 look at the processes you need to master to help your company and your salespeople successfully attain your mutual goals. We are still concerned with the motivational environment, but in these chapters, we examine how it fits into the overall selling system.

Chapter 6

Hiring New Salespeople

Building your sales team can help give your company a competitive edge, and the composition of your team begins with the hiring process. Hiring new salespeople is a responsibility all sales managers continually deal with, but the majority are not prepared to hire the best available candidate. Most sales managers approach hiring as an occasional event they have to suffer through.

You can maximize your hiring efforts by approaching it as a four-step process. The first step involves organizing and planning; before you can interview potential salespeople, you first need to decide on the salary range and minimum skill levels the new person needs to have. The second step is the interviewing process, and the third is writing a confirming letter of employment to quantify your job offer and job performance expectations. Step four involves planning for a strong first week at work to make sure your new hire starts off positively.

Step One: Organizing and Planning Your Hiring Strategy

One of the first decisions to make is how much you need to pay and what kinds of selling skills you are willing to accept for that salary. What skills do you want your next hire to have? What are the minimum skills and abilities you expect a new salesperson to bring to your company?

A management team that is working on a hiring strategy may begin with a planning session to list all the attributes desired in a new salesperson. After a great deal of discussion, the team members will probably develop a long list of preferences. Of course, these abilities can cost the company at least $150,000 per year in salary and commissions. Since management only wants to pay $40,000 to $50,000 a year (for example), the team will need to remove attributes from the list to create a more reasonable catalog of requirements that will fit the company's identified pay scale. After much effort, the team cuts down on some of its demands, but the list is probably still too long. Does this sound like your management team's expectations?

There is a common management assumption that a good interviewer can find and attract a salesperson who is skilled but does not know his or her true market value. This salesperson will therefore be happy to take whatever sounds like a reasonable offer. The reality is that sales managers are dealing with an efficient and elastic market when hiring a sales person. In the vast majority of cases, a salesperson attracted to a $40,000 job will tend to be, at best, a $40,000 salesperson. A $60,000 or $70,000 performer will not be attracted to the same types of opportunities. You make a major hiring mistake when you think you are hiring high-priced talent at a bargain rate. Look at this rationally: With all the sales jobs open, even in a tough economy, a person who is truly worth a high salary is able to get it. If you want a top performer, you will have to pay top dollar. Besides, if you did attract a salesperson at a "bargain salary," how long would he or she stay before being hired away by another, higher-paying company?

Skill Comfort Zones

One of the ways you can increase your chances of hiring a good salesperson is to better understand the components that make up an effective performer. There are three major skill comfort zones a salesperson can have. These categories are highlighted in Exhibit 6.1.

1. **People skills.** These skills give a person the ability to understand how to sell persuasively. How effective and persuasive are a candidate's communication skills? Has he or she ever sold anything before? How much sales training has he or she already had? These are all components of the comfort zone that deal with people skills. Someone who understands the steps of a sales call and how the persuasive selling process works will be comfortable in this category. Someone with these skills knows how to sell and deal persuasively with customers even if he or she has no experience selling within your industry or product area.

2. **Business or industry skills.** These skills translate into the ability to understand the uniqueness of customers' businesses within your

industry. Does the candidate understand your customers' financial business cycles, decision-making processes, and industry terminology? Someone with strong business or industry skills has experience selling to your type of customer, even if the goods he or she sold had nothing to do with your products or services.

3. **Technical or product skills.** Does the candidate understand how your products or services actually work? Is his or her technical product or application knowledge strong enough that your customers will recognize him or her as an expert who can successfully solve technical problems? Someone with strong technical or product skills has likely worked within your industry in another capacity, such as service or production. He or she is a technical expert who wants to move into selling.

Are the people you are interviewing already proven experts at selling, or are they knowledgeable about your industry? Are they technical experts? How much is a person with all three of these skills worth to you? How much could someone earn working for your direct competitor if he or she were experienced and effective in all three of these areas?

Since 99 percent of all sales managers and companies cannot afford someone with proven expertise in all three comfort zones, the next question is: How much are you willing to give up in each of these areas to get someone you can afford? Most sales manager evaluate potential salespeople backward by only focusing on the skills a candidate already has. A more effective interviewing style is to also focus on the skills lacking in the candidate. Keep this in mind: You will need to train this person once he or she is hired. Which of the candidate's weak areas are you most proficient in? Can you provide effective training to correct his or her deficiencies? It may be helpful to concentrate on these areas in your discussion.

Most sales managers have a natural bias toward a person who shares their comfort zone skills. If they are technical experts, they tend to like salespeople who exhibit the most technical knowledge during an interview. If they are strongest in selling and people skills, they lean toward someone who shares those attributes.

Building a sales team you can successfully coach and train requires you to think in opposite terms. If your strongest area is selling and people skills, you are most likely a good sales coach, but the other areas give you trouble. If your persuasive selling skills are your strength, would you not want to hire someone who has skills in the other areas you are weaker in? After all, you can easily teach him or her your strongest skills. Consider evaluating the next group of people you interview based on their people skills, industry skills, and technical knowledge. Decide how adept your new hire needs to be in each of these comfort zones. What is the minimum balance of skills you are willing to accept?

What is your bias? Which of the three categories is most difficult for you to train in your industry? There is no one right answer, but be careful: Most managers think the technical and industry aspects of their fields are the most difficult to learn; however, the ability to sell and persuade others is consistently the most difficult and time-consuming skill to learn.

Suppose you have two candidates for a sales position. One has a strong selling background but no experience with your product or industry; the other is a technical expert in your field and knows almost everything about your products but has never sold anything. Which of these candidates will have the shortest learning curve and generate the most sales revenues within the first year? There is no correct answer; however, even in the most technical industries, it is almost always easier and faster to teach an experienced salesperson technical information than it is to teach a technical expert selling and persuasion skills. What blend of comfort zones does your company need?

Company Appeal

Devising a successful hiring plan means not only evaluating what attributes you look for in a candidate, but what attributes a candidate looks for in you. A lot of managers forget that while they are interviewing to choose the best salesperson, interviewees are also assessing their company. Most managers never give much thought to selling their company to prospective hires. They are too busy focusing on which person they think will best fit

---

Team Leader's Tool

EVALUATING SALES POTENTIAL THE BEST WAY

When you determine a candidate's skills, ask yourself these four questions:

1. What are the minimum skills I am willing to accept in a new hire?
2. How much is a person with these skills worth to me?
3. How much is a person with these skills worth to my competitors?
4. If I cannot afford someone with expertise in all three comfort zones, which skill do I want to stress?

Do not let your personal bias trap you into hiring someone who shares your skills. Choose a person who is strong in another area but needs help in a comfort zone you can easily teach. Contrary to most companies' beliefs, technical skills have consistently proven to be the easiest to learn.

---

the job. The more attractive your company is, the more likely you will draw high-quality people who will want to stay with you.

To make your company more appealing, try looking at the situation from the prospective employee's standpoint. Joining a new organization is a significant risk for any salesperson. Salespeople ask themselves how much money they can make in their first few years, how hard it is to sell this company's products, how competitive the company is in the marketplace, and how enjoyable a place this will be to work. These are all difficult questions for a sales job interviewee to answer.

To strengthen your position with qualified candidates, consider developing three simple reports or brochures to give to each prospective salesperson you interview.

Benefit Report. This report details your company's working environment and covers pay plans and benefits. List exactly what kind of medical coverage your company offers. Describe the administrative and technical help available to each salesperson. Also detail the kind of management attention and help this salesperson can expect. If possible, describe the type of sales territory to which the person will be assigned and detail how much you plan to invest in first-year training, ongoing professional development, and coaching. Be specific about the kinds of sales training he or she will receive, concentrating on all three areas of persuasive selling skills, customer/industry skills, and product and technical knowledge. Show how much more comprehensive your company's training is for both entry-level and advanced salespeople compared to your competitors.

Average Success Report. One of the greatest difficulties for any salesperson is estimating how much he or she can earn in the first few years with a new company. This report lists the average incomes of your entire sales staff, including the highest and lowest numbers. List the average income earned during the first six months of employment, as well as the average after one and two years with the company. In an interview, most sales managers say things like, "If you're good and work hard, you can expect to sell about $400,000 worth of products and earn around $30,000 in your first full year." Compare the effect of this statement with the following: "You may want to look over this page of success averages for our sales force. This report shows that the average salesperson currently working for this company sold $412,000 of products during the first full year in his or her territory and earned an average of $31,000 in salary and commission." Which sounds more positive and more persuasive? Listing averages earned by your sales team is a strong persuasive tool. Since 90 percent of all salespeople feel they are above average, they will immediately assume they can outsell the other sales representatives in their first year, making your company and the sales job look even more attractive.

Unique Factor Grade Card Survey. This is a summary of surveys filled out by each of your current salespeople, showing what it is really like to work for your company. All sales managers interviewing prospective employees say how wonderful and unique their company is, but most of what they say is assumed by the candidate to be an exaggeration. By implementing a unique factor card survey process, you can prove to candidates what your present employees' opinions actually are. The survey is a subjective evaluation of your working environment. Questions can include:

- How nice is it to work here?
- How fair is this company?

- How much long-term potential do I have with this company?
- How much sales training and selling support do I receive?
- How competitive is this company within the market?
- How helpful and supportive is the sales management team?
- How much technical assistance and support do I receive?
- Am I respected and made to feel important by my company?

An example of a unique factor grade card is shown in Exhibit 6.2.

Any time you can quantify an idea, you give it strength and credibility. By conducting a unique factor survey of your existing sales force, you can have a fair and accurate evaluation of what it is like to work for you and your company. To have real impact, this survey needs to include both the strongest and weakest areas of your company. You will keep whoever you hire longer if you are open and give a complete picture of the environment, including the areas that need work. No one joining a new company is happy with surprises, especially negative ones.

For your survey to work, you first need to have a satisfied sales force. If you are experiencing a great deal of turnover and your sales environment has some serious problems, you may not want to use this idea. The survey concept only works when the rest of your company and managerial philosophies are stable and positive.

To successfully implement your survey, you first need to make sure the process is carefully planned and fully explained to your team before you distribute the form. Tell your salespeople the survey has two major goals. The first goal is to draw an accurate picture of your company to be used in interviewing new salespeople. The second goal is to help you and other sales managers understand how the sales representatives as a group feel about the company. Let them know you want to understand what changes or improvements they feel can help enhance the existing selling environment. If you have enough salespeople, it can improve the accuracy of your results if responses can be anonymous. Stress that comments will be summarized by an office assistant and that you will not see the individual pages. To improve the motivational environment of your company, have a group discussion with your sales team after the results have been summarized. Show your findings and ask for suggestions of ways to improve the existing environment.

Legal Considerations

A critical final step in the planning process is to talk to your company's personnel department or lawyer. Hiring laws are quite complex, and you leave yourself open to potential lawsuits if you are not fully aware of exactly what you may and may not ask in an interview.

STEP TWO: INTERVIEWING

After you have decided on an affordable pay range and the minimum skills you are willing to accept, the second step in the hiring process is interviewing. Interviewing a potential salesperson is exactly like conducting a normal, structured sales call; both consist of the following five steps (adapted for an interview):

1. Lower the candidate's resistance.
2. Ask questions to learn about the person and qualify your interest in him or her.
3. Present the features and benefits of your company and the available job.
4. Close to see if the candidate is interested in "buying" the job.
5. If interest exists, agree to your next call or appointment.

Most sales managers are already effective interviewers, but there are still some steps that can strengthen this phase of the hiring process. For example, if you are advertising for an available position, you can reduce the number of responses from inappropriate candidates by clearly stating your needs and expectations in your advertisement. Refer to the list you generated in the planning stage. The sample in Exhibit 6.3 will give you an idea of how to structure your ad. Be sure to include the following:

- Overall job responsibilities
- Your product or service
- Full-time or part-time status
- Benefits (including training, support, and environment) and projected earnings
- Necessary qualifications

To help save time when evaluating applicants, set up a procedure to screen for minimum skills or experience. You may want to have one of your support people conduct an initial interview by telephone. If the applicant exceeds your minimum requirements, the assistant schedules an appointment for him or her to meet with you for the first round of interviews.

When you interview someone, make sure you have them talk separately with at least two other people. This way, you will be able to discuss and evaluate each candidate with your coworkers, allowing you to get a clearer picture of the candidates since each person will likely see something different in each interviewee.

If at all possible, have the final two or three applicants come back for a second interview. A second round of interviews with at least three separate interviewers gives you a much better understanding and awareness of the candidates' potential. Most sales managers hire after only one round of interviews and do all the interviewing themselves. They invest more time and effort in purchasing a photocopier for their office than hiring a new salesperson.

After your initial round of interviews, be sure to check all references and past work experiences for each candidate. Some recent studies have found that up to 25 percent of all applicants use false or significantly misleading information on their resumes. Some will even list phony master's or doctorate degrees.

After narrowing your selection to one or two final applicants, offer to let them ride with one of your salespeople for a day to observe your company and job expectations. Olivia, a recent MBA graduate, went through several interviews with a large, prestigious international corporation that was headquartered in her hometown. After numerous meetings, the sales manager took her to lunch and presented her with a firm job offer. She was ready to say yes, but before he would accept her answer, the manager asked her to spend a day with one of his junior salespeople. He explained that he wanted to make sure she really understood what the job involved and what the company would expect from her before she was hired. A week later, Olivia spent the day riding with a junior salesperson. Within the first hour, she saw that no matter how prestigious the corporation, this was the worst job she could ever imagine. She was bored and ready to leave well before lunch. The job was nothing like her assumptions, and she knew she would never survive the two years necessary to be considered for a promotion. That evening the sales manager called to ask what she thought of the job and his company. Olivia apologized, but told him she could never enjoy or be successful in the type of environment he offered. Thinking she had let the manager and his company down, she was surprised when he thanked her for rejecting his offer. He said he was sorry she was not going to work out, but he would much rather find out now than after his company had spent thousands of dollars and several months training her for the position.

Have you ever hired someone, only to have them leave within a year because they were unhappy or dissatisfied with the job or your company? A day on the job will not guarantee a positive hire, but it may dramatically reduce the potential for an unproductive, unhappy salesperson who did not realize what he or she was getting into.

STEP THREE: WRITING THE CONFIRMING LETTER OF AGREEMENT

Once you have selected your final candidate and are ready to make a job offer, it is time to put the offer in writing. There are many details involved in offering someone a job. A hiring letter of agreement allows you to explain to your new salesperson exactly what you offer and what you expect. This letter is not meant to be a contract; it is a statement that describes the rules and procedures your company expects the person to follow when joining your sales team.

It is amazing how a candidate can misconstrue a job offer. The real advantage of a letter of employment comes when — three months after joining your company — your new salesperson selectively remembers your original offer. A detailed letter allows you to eliminate the gray areas that may cause hassles or hurt feelings later.

If you use any type of employment letter, make sure your lawyer or personnel department has a chance to review it. There is no standard format for such a letter, but some of the important areas to cover include:

- Company rules and procedures
- Starting salary and commission rates
- Medical benefits
- Minimum performance expectations
- Specific territory and quota assignments
- Minimum standards for evaluation
- Minimum standards of ethics and professionalism
- Agreement to allow you to train and coach the new person
- Employee rights
- Starting date

Both the manager and the new salesperson need to sign this letter and keep copies to prevent serious disagreements in the future.

STEP FOUR: PLANNING THE FIRST WEEK OF WORK

Remember your first week in the last job you started? The first few days in any new job are stressful and uncomfortable. It is your job as the new person's sales manager to make sure that his or her first week is as productive and busy as possible. This sounds simple, but many companies hire new people and then leave them with nothing to do for a week because the sales manager is busy handling a crisis.

Consider assigning a guide or host for your new hire for the first several days until he or she is comfortable with the company. You may also want to prepare a list of activities for the new person's first few weeks — the goal is to get your new hire productively involved in the new environment quickly.

It is also important to realize that orientation continues throughout a salesperson's first year of working for your company. The senior salesperson who served as the new hire's guide for the first week can also be a positive nonmanagerial mentor who can help him or her understand your company's culture. You may also want to give your new sales representative a mini-performance review after the first week on the job. Repeat the meeting once a month for six months to be sure that you are happy with the salesperson's performance and that he or she understands how he or she is doing.

TEAM LEADER'S TOOL

HELPING NEW HIRES THROUGH THE FIRST WEEK OF WORK

The following suggestions can make your new salespeople feel comfortable and can help them adjust to their new job:

- If you are a smaller company, consider making a book that includes snapshots, names, department, and job responsibilities of each person in the company. New hires will be able to quickly learn other employees' names and how they fit into the organization.
- Arrange several private lunches or breakfasts with executives, department managers, and senior employees. This allows key individuals to offer suggestions and guidance to new sales representatives.
- Have your new hires spend a day in each of the major departments they will be working with. This gives them a better understanding of the staff they will interface with once they begin selling.
- Make sure you give new salespeople solid feedback — both positive and negative — on their job performance throughout their first few months. Many sales managers who believe their new people are doing a good job never say anything or provide encouragement.
- Have new salespeople interview as many of your current representatives as possible. This can give new hires a broader insight into the selling environment and help your entire sales force become acquainted with new team members.
- Remember that you have hired these people for sales positions. Keep your training and the issues you discuss balanced between the three areas of selling, information controls and business practices, and technical areas. Many companies hire salespeople and spend the first few weeks of employment dealing with product issues instead of sales-focused issues.

SUMMARY

To reduce hiring "mistakes" and to bring in the best talent every time, organize and plan your efforts before you begin to interview applicants. Make sure several people interview each serious candidate, and when your decision is made, draft a confirming letter of employment for you and the new hire to sign. As a final step in the hiring process, carefully plan the first few weeks of activities that will make the new salesperson comfortable in your environment and eager to achieve.

Hiring new salespeople is only one of a sales manager's responsibilities. The next chapter examines ways to handle communication within the sales environment.

EXHIBIT 6.1 SKILL COMFORT ZONES FOR SALESPEOPLE

People Skills

The ability to understand how to sell persuasively

Questions:
- How effective and persuasive are the candidate's communication skills?
- How much sales *experience* has this person had?
- How much sales *training* has this person had?

Business or Industry Skills

The ability to understand the uniqueness of customers' businesses within your industry

Questions:
- Does the candidate understand your industry's business cycles?
- Is the candidate familiar with industry terminology?
- Does the candidate understand your customers' decision-making cycles?

Technical or Product Skills

The ability to understand how your products or services really work

Questions:
- Does this person understand in detail how your products or services work?
- Is this person's technical and application knowledge strong enough for your customers to recognize him or her as a technical expert?
- Can this candidate successfully solve your customers' technical problems?

EXHIBIT 6.2 SAMPLE UNIQUE FACTOR GRADE CARD

1 ·······2········3·········4 ·······**5** ·······6·········7·········8·········9 ·····**10**

| **Very Bad** | **Neutral** | **Fantastic** |

1. How nice a place is this to work?

_____Coworkers' attitudes toward you

_____Management's attitude toward you

_____Customers' attitudes toward you

_____Service department's attitude toward you

2. How fair is this company?

_____Fairness of commission plan

_____Fairness of commission plan administration

_____Fairness of raises and promotions

_____Fairness of territory assignments

_____Fairness of my success potential and future opportunities with this company

3. How much potential do I have with this company?

_____The opportunity to double my income within the next 12 months

_____The amount of support and help from management in my work

_____Management's wish for me to be successful and make as much money as possible

_____The company's ability to offer me opportunities to be successful for the next 10 years

_____The opportunity for a promotion path to management

4. What kind of training and selling support do I receive?

_____Effectiveness of this company's selling and people skill training

_____Effectiveness of this company's business or industry skill training

_____Effectiveness of management's support of me and my selling efforts

_____Effectiveness and cooperation of service department with me and my customers

_____Effectiveness and cooperation of office staff with me and my customers

EXHIBIT 6.2
(CONTINUED)

5. What is this company's impact from my customers' perspective?

_____Effectiveness of our service department

_____Effectiveness of our order entry department and product delivery

_____Effectiveness of our billing and accounts receivable departments

_____Quality of our product line and inventory

_____Uniqueness of our product line

_____Ease of our return policy

_____Effectiveness of our credit department

_____Effectiveness of our pricing

_____Effectiveness of our large customer pricing policies

6. [Add your own questions]

_____**Total**

EXHIBIT 6.3 SAMPLE ADVERTISEMENT

Are You an Experienced Selling Professional?

Experienced telephone professional wanted to sell speaking and consulting services of a nationally-known sales and persuasion consultant.
This is a full-time position contacting major corporations and associa-
tions across the U.S. Excellent draw/commission plan. Full training
offered on a proven low pressure marketing system that really works.
Job offers comfortable environment, medical benefits, full management
and word processing support. Annual commissions of $25,000 to
$50,000 probably within 12 to 18 months for an individual with
proven selling experience and high energy. Success qualifications: Be a
hard worker and quick learner; possess persuasive and professional
telephone voice. For consideration, call 919/555-3684.

CHAPTER 7

FORMAL AND INFORMAL COMMUNICATIONS

In previous chapters, we discussed how your managerial style can significantly affect the motivational environment of your salespeople. How you manage the information flows and paperwork of your organization can have an equally pivotal role. We have talked about how critical it is for you, as a sales manager, to effectively blend your positive and negative communications. But enhancing your company's information flow requires more than positive statements to your sales representatives. How efficient and effective are the communications within your organization?

Evaluating your company's information flows requires measuring the quality, quantity, and focus of both written and verbal communications between you, your salespeople, customers, and upper management. These messages can be either formal or informal. When did you last analyze all the information flows you are responsible for?

INFORMAL COMMUNICATIONS

Informal communication between you and your sales force is most effective when carried out daily. If you speak to your people infrequently, your eventual conversations will take on a more formal tone. The more formal your communications with your staff, the less of a coach and confidante you will be. How much informal communication and feedback do each of your salespeople need from you to help them build their own motivational environment? A basic communication rule is that the more informal the communication, the more accurate, open, and frequent the information exchange becomes.

Your working relationship with each of your salespeople is significantly influenced by how you communicate informally with them. These informal conversations need to be more than just personal chats. They need to include both positive and negative feedback about the job you feel your salesperson is doing. You also need to cover important account updates and potential actions that can help advance a sale. Ongoing client and competitor updates are also an important part of your informal communications.

The goal of informal communication is to give your people positive affirmations as you gain accurate, updated information on their selling activities. Are you consistently accomplishing this goal? Increasing the effectiveness of your communications does not need to take a great deal of time. One way is to always include at least one or two positive, yet honest and accurate, comments in every conversation. Visualize an old-fashioned balancing scale. If you need to give a salesperson several negative comments, what can you do to balance the other side of the scale with positive feedback?

A major problem in managing people is that everyone demands different information and management. There is no easy way to tell how much informal communication will benefit each person most. Some salespeople are motivated by an ongoing daily dialog with their manager, whereas others react more positively to a feeling of independence from their manager. Most experienced sales managers think they have already identified the ideal amount of informal communication for each of their people. They believe their experience is the best gauge. Although your experience with your people is critical to your success, you may want to consider asking each of your representatives to give you feedback on the effectiveness of your communications. As simple as this sounds, discussions about how to enhance working communications are rare.

FORMAL COMMUNICATIONS

Formal communications are comments that are "on the record" for you and others in your company to evaluate and review. One example is a letter you write to your salespeople and copy to others in the company. When one of your salespeople closes a large order, as a part of your feedback, you may give him or her a letter that lists all the positive actions he or she made to win the new business. The vice president of sales is copied on the letter, and another copy gets filed in the salesperson's permanent record. Formal feedback has the most impact when it is in writing and is combined with informal verbal communication. What types of formal communication do you have with your sales force?

Written formal communications include hiring letters of employment, which we covered in Chapter 6; territory coverage definitions that identify the accounts or geographic areas for which a salesperson is responsible; pay plans defining and quantifying how and when commissions and bonuses are paid; and annual or semiannual employee performance plans. How many of these formal written documents do you use regularly? The more of them you currently have in place, the fewer hassles and surprises you are likely to have as you work with your people.

For example, Steve, a sales manager from a small midwestern manufacturer, was the only sales manager in the company and had seven full-time salespeople reporting to him. He said his company had no real formal communications with the sales force because it was too small to require such communications. He said, "All my salespeople are paid on straight commission and know what is expected of them and what they have to do." The salespeople had no formal quota assignments, but Steve said quotas were unnecessary because his team was motivated by the desire to earn a lot of money. Does Steve's situation sound familiar? Consider the circumstances for a moment. Can he keep running his department without any formal communication structures? Of course, but without written "benchmarks," he leaves himself and his company open to future challenges and disagreements from the sales force that could severely weaken the motivational environment.

Formal communication instruments prevent surprises. Written documents allow everyone to agree on exactly what is expected for the next several months or years. This is important because most people are selective listeners; we hear and remember only what we want to. Suppose you have a two-hour meeting with one of your people in which you discuss how commissions are paid, the available bonuses, territory assignments, and what you expect this person to accomplish over the next year. You are giving him or her the opportunity to second guess and challenge you in the future if there is nothing in writing that summarizes what was covered in the meeting.

The three most critical formal information documents for sales management success are written annual quota assignments, annual written detailed definitions of sales territory assignments, and annual or semiannual employee performance plans.

Written Annual Quota Assignments

Are your salespeople assigned annual quotas — in writing — that identify how much you expect them to sell within the next business year? If not, you may be setting yourself and your company up for lower sales and a less-than-motivated sales staff.

Two sales managers in a heavy equipment company said they each managed a salesperson who underperformed compared to the rest of the sales team. This company paid straight commissions, and at the beginning of the year, the managers asked each salesperson to identify how much money he or she wanted to make for the year and to quantify how much he or she would need to sell to reach that personal goal. The two low performers had been setting financial goals in the low $30,000 income range for the past several years. Although both representatives reached their personal goals, their sales managers and company executives were unhappy because they believed both people could sell twice as much. The other representatives were making $50,000 or more. Because everyone had an assigned territory, the managers felt they were losing valuable territory coverage, and that the two low performers were not working up to their full potential. The company judged that each salesperson received the same amount of sales support and sales management time as everyone else, but they generated only half the profit. The sales management team tried to decide how to get these people to sell to their full potential. Each sales manager had spoken to them several times, but the representatives' attitude was, "I'm on 100 percent commission, so what does it matter how much I sell as long as I'm happy with my income?"

This example illustrates one of the most significant problems in neglecting to set annual sales quotas. When you have no assigned annual quota or sales goals, there is no way for you to object to your team's production or lack thereof. A sales manager's job is to help people achieve more than they thought they could. Assigning annual quotas is one way to do this. A large part of managing salespeople with quotas is to help them focus and believe in their own expectations. It has consistently been proven that whatever you truly believe is impossible to achieve will be impossible to achieve. There is no way you can accomplish something you know to be impossible. It is a normal part of human behavior to want to prove all your expectations correct. How are you helping define a higher level of expectations in your salespeople?

Sales Quota Program Goals. An effective sales quota program has three goals. The first is to select a sales quota that requires your salesperson to work a little harder and be more creative about overall selling efforts. A suitable sales quota helps stretch people into selling more than they expected.

The second goal is to make sure the quota is believable. It will only be productive when your sales representatives believe they have a reasonable, reachable assignment. How much can you increase a salesperson's quota without making it seem impossible? Unfortunately, there is no one correct percentage increase. But the more facts you supply (supported by extensive discussion and coaching) to prove that a new quota is possible, the more likely the team will accept your idea of a "fair stretch."

The third and final goal of an effective sales quota is perceived fairness. Your team needs to see whatever number you set as fair and balanced. It is acceptable to assign higher numbers to your senior people, but the entire sales force needs to feel there is a balance and overall fairness to the final quotas. People who feel their personal quotas require them to work harder than any of their teammates will be less motivated. Once a quota system has been in place for a few years, many companies assign a new quota based on a percentage increase over the previous year's quota or sales figures. It is difficult for a salesperson to feel a new quota is unfair if all representatives are given a volume sales goal that is, for instance, 12 percent higher than their last year's performance.

Another element of perceived quota fairness is based on how a new quota will affect compensation. If part of the team's compensation is based on their quota attainment, this increase should be tied to a similar increase in bonus dollars. One services company paid its salespeople a salary plus a sales bonus. The bonus was based on annual sales but was measured on year-to-date quarterly sales production. Because the company wanted to focus on achieving 100 percent of assigned sales quotas, management used an exponential bonus program, which is calculated by multiplying the appropriate bonus dollars by the percent of quota of achieved and again by the percent of quota achieved. Thus, any quota achieved has a double impact. Someone performing below his or her quota receives a significantly lower bonus than someone who overperforms. For example, if the sales bonus is $10,000 and a salesperson comes in at 90 percent for the year, under the exponential bonus program, he or she earns $8,100 (90% × 90% = 81% × $10,000). If that same person comes in at 75 percent for the year, he or she would earn a bonus of only $5,600. However, if he or she finished at 115 percent, $13,200 would be paid.

The benefit of this type of bonus program is that you pay much less to your lower performers and have a built-in accelerated bonus program for anyone who goes over his or her quota. Although the calculations sound rather complex, it is a simple way to offer a single bonus program that ensures your best performers a significantly higher bonus than your lowest performers. Many companies like the exponential bonus program because it offers a fair way to direct more bonus dollars to top performers, and, once you walk your people through the calculations, it is an easy program to understand and manage. No matter what type of bonus program you use, it is critical that any increase in quota be bound to a similar increase in bonus dollars. If you expect more from your salespeople, they will expect more earning potential. This is easily accomplished if you pay straight commissions, but it becomes more difficult when you pay a combination of salary plus commission or salary plus bonus. We discuss the relative benefits and consequences of various pay plans in Chapter 11.

Implementing a Quota Program. The first step in implementing a successful quota system begins prior to the sales year in question. Before you can start working with your salespeople on setting quotas, you need to first decide how much you think each of them will achieve during the next year. This can either be defined as a gross sales figure or as a percentage increase over last year's levels. To help ensure your quotas will achieve the three goals of stretch, believability, and fairness, consider preparing your own detailed forecast of how and where you feel each person can produce sales. Assigning successful sales quotas requires accuracy in identifying the increased sales volume management requires with an awareness of the reality of possible production numbers for your sales team.

Once you have identified achievable quota levels, the second step in the process is to position your sales team's expectations. Approximately 30 days before the end of the current year, ask your people to prepare individual forecasts showing what they think they can sell next year. Have them list, by account, what they feel they can accomplish and tell them their forecasts need to surpass last year's numbers. Give them the percentage increase over the previous year that you expect them to work with. This working forecast number needs to be equal to or a little higher than the actual quota you plan to assign. The purpose of this exercise is to start your people believing that next year's sales numbers need to be higher than this year's.

Offer your help to anyone who feels there is no way he or she can sell even close to last year's numbers. If you work with them, they will either prove to you they need a quota exception, or you will prove to them the validity of your increased performance expectations. This is also a good time to begin informally discussing with each person the achievability of higher sales during the next year. It is important to allow your people time to verbalize any concerns or resistance they have. This is also a good time to begin discussing what changes they plan to make to their personal selling styles, selling approaches, and account coverage plans to help them increase their total sales in the coming year.

Step three in setting a quota is to pass out quota assignments as close to the first day of the new year as possible. This is best accomplished in a group meeting where everyone can see what everyone's new assignments are. Be sure to put all quota assignments in writing. If quotas have to be passed out individually because of geographic constraints, putting them in writing and distributing them to all your people at the same time will reinforce their fairness and equality. But do not get ahead of yourself: It is important to assign new quotas after the start of the year. Assigning them before the end of the current year may distract people from their present goals and even cause some of them to delay or hide orders until the new year.

A critical aspect of distributing new quota assignments is your ability to manage the perceptions and emotions of your sales team. There is a strong possibility that, even with the positioning you did in step two, a few of your people will feel their new numbers are unrealistic or unfair. This is a good time for you to explain why you feel each salesperson can achieve his or her newly assigned quota. It is important to meet privately after the meeting with anyone who is upset.

The executive team of a medical equipment company decided the organization needed significantly higher quotas for the coming year. Past year increases had averaged between 7 percent and 11 percent and the following year's increase would be 15 percent over the previous year's quotas. To minimize the impact of the new quotas, in mid-December, the sales managers mentioned they had heard from the executive staff that numbers were going to be much higher the following year. These preliminary informal comments conditioned the sales team to anticipate a different level of performance expectation. The new quotas were the most important issue at the company's mid-January kickoff meeting, which opened with a review of the previous year and a presentation of expectations for the coming year. The executives said the company's new product line had significant advantages over the competition, and hospital budgets for applications looked much stronger in the near future. After the quotas were distributed, the sales managers met with their teams to discuss the changes. Each salesperson received a paper listing how the manager felt he or she could achieve 100 percent of his or her new quota. The paper also showed how much each person's income would increase when the new quota was met. The managers then repeated their commitment to helping each of their people achieve their new numbers. Finally, as a group, the teams debated the benefits and consequences of complaining to showing a positive attitude to executives.

During the next two days of the meeting, executive team members made sure they were accessible to the representatives to give them a chance to comment on the expected difficulties of their new assignments. After the kickoff meeting, the sales managers had extensive private discussions with each of their people to help them see the new quotas as a positive opportunity instead of a negative demotivator. Thanks to all of these efforts, combined with ongoing coaching and training, the majority of salespeople successfully achieved their assigned quotas.

Be aware that the greater the quota increase, the more important it is for you to discuss the situation both formally and informally with your

---

TEAM LEADER'S TOOL

ESTABLISHING A SUCCESSFUL QUOTA PLAN

Follow these four steps to set up an effective quota plan:

1. Before a new sales year begins, decide how much you think each salesperson will be able to achieve during the next year. You can define the goal as either a gross sales figure or as a percentage increase over the previous year.

2. Position your sales team's expectations. About a month before the end of the sales year, ask them to prepare individual forecasts showing how much they think they can sell in the coming year. Remind them to forecast by account, and emphasize your expectation that their new forecast needs to be higher than the previous year's performance.

3. At a group meeting, distribute written quota assignments as close to the first day of the new year as possible. If quotas have to be assigned individually, put them in writing and pass them out to all your people at the same time. To manage your team's perceptions and emotions, explain why you feel they can make their newly assigned quotas. Remind them that you are on their side, and that it is your job to help them reach their goals. Ask for feedback and allow some time for discussion. The greater the quota increase, the greater the need for you to hear your team's positive and negative reactions. Meet privately with anyone who is still upset after the meeting.

4. Stay in constant contact with your people. Keep checking to see how they feel about their new quotas and find out what they are doing to ensure that they meet their numbers.

---

people and listen to their concerns. This is also an important time for you to remind them that you are on their side and that your job is to help them meet their numbers. Remind them that your success as a sales manager depends on their success in making their quotas. End the discussion by talking about how they can change to achieve their quotas. During these discussions, it is also critical to show empathy and compassion for your people. The more stressed and concerned a salesperson is, the more sensitivity and understanding you need to show. It is okay for you to agree that a new quota may seem like an unfair stretch. You can then ask your team what they can do to ensure a committed attempt at success.

The fourth step in setting successful quotas is to stay in constant contact with your people. Keep checking in with them to see how they feel about their quotas and what they are doing to make their numbers for the year.

Written Detailed Definitions of Sales Territory Assignments

In addition to written quota assignments, the second formal information document that functions as a coaching tool is a written definition of sales territory assignment. This is a simple document that details exactly what territory a salesperson is to cover. You may assign territories by state, zip code, or industry or product type. Most definitions of assignments list the assigned accounts, their addresses, and any relevant customer information such as customer numbers or existing contractual information. The area of new account prospecting expected is also usually included. If you have several salespeople in the same geographical area, you may assign what are called *open territories,* in which any prospect is open for any salesperson. Under an open territory arrangement, an account is only formally assigned to a salesperson after he or she has begun calling on a company or has sold something.

There are two reasons to prepare definitions of territory assignments. The first is to remove any confusion or misunderstanding about handling prospects and new business. The second is to ensure that your sales representatives understand what specific accounts they are responsible for. A leading problem of unassigned territories is the potential to ignore solid prospects that could develop into new customers or to ignore existing customers who are difficult or overly demanding. Whether the territory is geographic or involves assigned accounts, each salesperson has a responsibility to work the entire territory and to identify all major potential selling opportunities, both existing or new, within his or her area. Written definitions of sales territory assignments identify full territory account responsibilities, and your ongoing coaching helps ensure that salespeople sell to their full territories throughout the year. Written account assignments also ensure that all your existing accounts have a salesperson assigned to support their requirements.

Employee Performance Plans

An employee performance plan is a written document you develop with each of your people. It is a detailed listing of each representative's goals and expectations over a specific period of time. The majority of performance plans cover one year and are tied to the beginning and end of the sales quota period.

When it is completed at the beginning of the year, a performance plan serves as a tactical guide for the salesperson and as a coaching tool for the sales manager. Most plans include a description of the sales territory assignment, quotas to be achieved, specific account sales goals, and personal development objectives.

The best employee performance plans involve extensive planning and development at the beginning of the year, several informal reviews and progress discussions during the year, and an end-of-year formal review of accomplishments and areas to be worked on during the next period. Semiannual written performance plans are also effectively used when there is a tremendous change in sales territories or product lines, when a salesperson is underperforming and/or is on probation, or when a representative is new to selling or to an assigned territory.

Planned Goals. An effective performance plan can be a major contributor to the sales team's motivational environment. There are several goals or objectives for the plan.

A performance plan provides an ongoing vehicle to help open the lines of communication between you and your salespeople about your expectations and goals for the coming year. Performance plans involve your salespeople in the discussion of continuous self-improvement and encourage them to be part of the goal-setting process. It is a way of looking at the entire upcoming year and your employees' work goals and expectations in one discussion.

A performance plan also provides you with an excellent measurement tool for each salesperson. It furnishes a mechanism to document, correct, or eliminate unacceptable behavior or below-standard performance levels. Performance plans give you and your people a format in which to discuss both the positive and negative aspects of their performance. Multiple years of written performance plans give you a solid basis for evaluating promotion qualifiers and/or underperformers who are not making the grade.

The most important benefit of performance plans is that they help you and your salesperson identify how you both can change to enhance his or her selling environment and working conditions. The most successful performance plan programs involves two-way communications and coaching between you and your people. One communication direction is you as coach and advisor to your salesperson. Another equally important communication direction is for your salesperson to give you feedback on the kind of job he or she feels you are doing for him as a manager. Allowing your people to give you input provides a tremendous feeling of empowerment and importance to your sales team.

There are potential problems even when a performance plan is properly implemented. One of these problems arises if you do not follow through with your role in the process. If you put a strong set of expectations in writing for salespeople and they meet and significantly exceed those expectations, you need to be prepared to somehow recognize their accomplishments with bonuses, rewards, raises, or increased benefits.

A performance plan program can be seen as a demotivator if it is perceived as time consuming, complex, arbitrary, impersonal, overly bureaucratic, or unfair. Most large corporate programs are ineffective one-way communication tools used by sales managers to lecture salespeople about negatives and inadequacies of the past year's performance. These plans are only a report card that leave no room for the employee's thoughts or feelings. This type of plan ultimately does more damage than good to the motivational environment of the sales force.

Program Implementation. It takes extensive preparation to implement a successful performance program in a company. First, you need to decide what important employee performance areas need to be measured. You and your fellow managers need to agree on a consistent set of performance expectations for your entire sales force. Most plans divide employee measurement into six major categories. Several personal action items or goals are then identified for each category.

1. The first and most important category is *business volume and product objectives.* This category identifies assigned quotas and expected selling volumes of individual product or service offerings. Specific sales objectives of major accounts and/or new business generation expectations can also be defined.

2. The second major category is *marketing objectives,* which covers how sales representatives are expected to make their quotas. Use of company resources or staff is defined, as well as how and when the salesperson is expected to request help from management on important sales calls or critical customer situations. In this category, you explain how you will support and coach the salesperson. It includes your commitments, responsibilities, and accessibility.

3. The third category of a performance plan is *territory management objectives.* This category outlines how a salesperson is expected to manage his or her territory and selling efforts. This is where you define specific territory assignments, listed by geography or individual account listings. Budgets and spending expectations fall into this category. You also want to ensure that all reports and forecasts submitted by the salesperson will be complete, accurate, and timely. Maximum outstanding accounts receivable and the representative's involvement in payment collection may also be quantified. Territory

management expectations for the salesperson may be outlined here, and need to include specifications of anticipated productivity and efficiency improvements.

4. The fourth category is *customer satisfaction objectives,* which delineates how a salesperson is expected to manage minimum customer service standards and dealings with the competition or dissatisfied customers.

5. The fifth major category, *personal and professional development objectives,* defines the values and behavior you expect from your salesperson. This is where you stress the importance of a positive attitude and being a team player. You also cover how each salesperson needs to communicate and deal with support staff, customers, and the management team. This category emphasizes your company's commitment to ongoing training and skill improvement. You may focus on personalized expectations for individual improvement in areas such as product knowledge, industry or business skills, time management, and persuasive selling skills. You can also target completion of specific training programs, books, or self-study tapes.

6. The sixth major category is *additional plans and responsibilities.* This category allows you or your salesperson to identify any additional behaviors, skills, or actions to be improved during the coming year. Some companies also include career development and promotion expectations in this category. Others will identify expected industry or community involvement or assistance with coaching junior salespeople.

After you have identified the areas and levels of employee performance to measure, the next step is to meet with all your group of people to explain the entire program. The purpose of this meeting is to show the team why and how a performance plan program will benefit them. You may want to say something like, "This plan will give you a clearer understanding of my expectations of you. It will also allow you to be a part of the planning process that sets your annual goals and expectations." You need to explain that a performance plan is first and foremost a communication tool. It will not directly decide pay raises or promotions. Consistent performance may eventually earn team members a raise, but a successful performance plan evaluation will not guarantee one. At the end of the meeting, ask each sales-person to write up his or her plans and expectations for the year. Tell them you will do the same for each of them and will want to meet individually to finalize their personal performance plans. The outline in Exhibit 7.1 states major categories and actions and/or goals that your people should include in their plans. Be sure to stress that performance plans are best stated in outline form. This is not meant to be a 30-page term paper. Emphasize that each line item needs to be concise and to the point.

Exhibit 7.2 is a sample performance plan that has been filled out for a fictitious sales representative. In this sample, the five-point rating scale has been used. Each section has three columns: the first is filled out at the beginning of the year with plans for achievements/improvements; the second is completed at the end of the year and states what has (or has not) been achieved; and the third column leaves space for ranking each point.

The next step in implementing a performance plan program involves a one-on-one meeting with each salesperson. In this meeting, stress that the plan is completely personal and confidential. Walk through each major category in the outline with your salesperson. It is critical to discuss what needs to be included in each category. The plan will only be an effective coaching tool if salespeople agree with all the expectations and have had meaningful input. At the conclusion of this meeting, you will have a hand-written, detailed performance plan. You and the salesperson should then sign the plan, showing agreement with the contents and the importance of following the plan expectations throughout the coming year. Make a pho-tocopy of the signed handwritten plan for the salesperson before he or she leaves. Follow up with a typed copy that both of you sign. Each of you then retains a signed final typed copy of the personal plan.

Now that a formal performance plan exists for each of your salespeo-ple, you have a tool to reference during your ongoing coaching sessions. The most effective plans are informally reviewed and discussed as often as once a month. It is important that all of your people feel they can bring up or reference their plan at any time so that positive actions or accom-plishments can be noted. Also, plan to update or modify specific plans as the environment or territory changes. A performance plan is best used as a working document between you and the representative, not as an unchanging list of absolutes. Most large corporate performance plans are ineffective because they are written by management (with no employee involvement) and are reviewed only briefly in a one-way "management-does-all-the-talking" meeting. They are also ignored and never mentioned during the year. The salesperson is then harshly evaluated at the end of the year because he or she accomplished so few of the assigned responsibilities or goals.

The last step in implementing a successful employee performance plan involves the end-of-year review. This meeting has two goals: to review and discuss the salesperson's accomplishments and activities during the past year and to develop a personalized performance plan for the coming year.

When it is time to review and close out a performance plan, ask the sales representative to prepare for the annual performance review by outlining how he or she rates his or her performance over the past year, identifying achievements for the various items on the original plan. Have him or her begin preparing a detailed plan for the coming year as well.

At the same time, you will prepare your final review of the salesperson, noting next year's quota expectations and adjustments to the upcoming plan. You may consider using either a three- or five-point ranking system, both of which are shown in Exhibit 7.3. Quantifying each action item of a performance plan allows you and the salesperson a better understanding of his or her final performance rating. A ranking is assigned to each line or action item of a performance plan, and the total of these numbers summarizes the person's general performance. Any low-ranking item necessitates an action plan to immediately correct it. You may wish to use formal probation if the problem is integral to overall sales levels or job performance. Once these rankings are done individually, meet to review them with the representative, restating the two goals of reviewing and closing out last year's performance plan and agreeing to the contents of next year's plan.

Begin by letting the salesperson give his or her general comments and observations for the year just completed. After you have made your comments, work through the past year's performance plan, ranking each line item as you go. It is critical that you and the salesperson have already rated each item. If you scored the same number for a particular area, the discussion can be kept to a minimum and you can move on to the next line. Detailed, lengthy discussions are necessary only when you and the salesperson have a different ranking assigned to a certain item. Put your comments in writing ahead of time so you have a reference.

As you lead the meeting, it is important to balance talk about positive achievements and areas that need improvement. The more negative the performance review meeting, the less beneficial the overall plan. Remember that a performance plan is a big-picture coaching tool to help maximize the salesperson's motivational environment. It is not a disciplinary tool. If a salesperson's behavior is truly negative or unacceptable during the year, respond immediately — do not wait until the end-of-year review to let the person know you are unhappy with his or her performance.

To complete the performance review, you and your salesperson need to write down final comments and observations. Both of you then date and sign the final document. The original goes in the employee's file, and the salesperson retains a copy.

The performance review is an excellent opportunity to discuss the person's long-term career goals and expectations. What are his or her objectives? Where does he or she want to be in 5 or 10 years?

Before you begin working on the following year's plan, the review also presents a good opportunity to ask for feedback concerning your performance as a sales manager over the last year. Ask for observations and suggestions concerning your behavior and your management style. What do your people feel you do best? Where do you need improvement over the next year? What would they most like to see you change that could improve their ability to meet their sales quotas and objectives? Also ask them for an evaluation of the company and the sales support from other departments. What changes or improvements would increase their productivity or selling success? Remember that you do not have to act on everything they say. It is also important to stay calm and not take any suggestions too personally. The goal is to get input. You will destroy this environment if you appear overly sensitive or defensive in your responses to suggestions or feedback. The goal of two-way feedback is to learn each other's concerns and work on improvements where they are practical.

A salesperson's assessment of sales management efforts is a critical component to building an effective sales team. How can a person feel you are working together if all evaluations and feedback proceed only in one direction? Sales managers who seek feedback say they get a lot of great suggestions that improve the overall working environment for their sales force. When was the last time you asked your people to evaluate your managerial efforts?

After you solicit feedback on your performance as a sales manager, identify what needs to be covered in next year's performance plan.

SUMMARY

Maintaining regular, informal exchanges with your salespeople is an effective way of strengthening your relationships and uncovering essential facts about their territories and accounts. Three formal communication documents also play an important role in your management efforts and deserve your attention: annual quota assignments, sales territory assignments, and annual employee performance plans.

Managing information flows consists not only of informal and formal communication between you and your people, but the paperwork that you deal with in your organization. Chapter 8 focuses on ways to manage this overwhelming specific type of information flow.

Exhibit 7.1 Suggested Components of an Employee Performance Plan

Section 1 Business Volumes and Product Objectives

Define minimum quotas

Define expected or required product unit sales

Quantify new account expectations and minimum sales volumes

Section 2 Marketing Objectives

Define proactive selling expectations

Define use of company resources

Identify importance of maintaining and improving customer satisfaction for new and existing customers

Define executive calling expectations

Section 3 Territory Management Objectives

Define territory boundaries or account assignments

Define importance of minimizing lost business

Define maximum expense ranges or expectations

Define territory reporting systems and information flows required, including forecasts and report deadlines

Define accurate report expectations

Define expected productivity and efficiency improvements

Minimize levels of outstanding accounts receivable

Section 4 Customer Satisfaction Objectives

Define minimum customer service standards

Identify need for quick customer problem identification and positive resolution

Identify importance of keeping your management team informed and updated on all significant account problems

Section 5 Personal and Professional Development Objectives

Stress importance of being a team player, positive role model, and professional company representative

Identify personal areas to be developed and education plans to facilitate them (Specify skills in the areas of selling, communication, time management, product knowledge, and industry and business knowledge.)

Identify expectations of honesty, ethical behavior, and integrity at all times

Section 6 Additional Plans and Responsibilities

Identify other behaviors, skills, or actions to be worked on

Identify longer-term plans and goals for career development and promotion

EXHIBIT 7.2 SAMPLE EMPLOYEE PERFORMANCE PLAN

Performance Plan for: Jane Hill

Begun: 12/16/XX **Completed:** 12/15/XX

Section 1: Business Volumes and Product Objectives

A. Define minimum quotas
B. Define expected or require product unit sales
C. Quantify new account expectations and minimum sales volumes

Plan	Results Achieved	Ranking
A. *19XX Assigned Quota* $750,000 equipment $50,000 maintenance contract revenue	• $800,000 equipment sales (107% of quota) • $35,000 maintenance contract revenue (70% of quota)	3
B. *Specific Product Sales Goals* • Sell and install a minimum of five new X120 models • Sell and install a minimum of ten X100 models	• Sold and successfully installed six X120s • Sold and installed only five X100s	2
C. Develop at least five new accounts in territory, produc-ing a minimum of 10% of quota from new customer sales	• Sold seven new accounts and generated $100,000 in new customer sales (13% of assigned quota)	4

Section 1 overall ranking: 3

Section 2: Marketing Objectives

D. Define proactive selling expectations
E. Define use of company resources
F. Identify importance of maintaining and improving customer satisfaction for new and existing customers
G. Define executive calling expectations

Plan	Results Achieved	Ranking
D. Maintain a proactive control of all selling opportunities and situations, properly planning, forecasting, and completing selling objectives assigned for the year	• Successfully completed for the most part • Still need work on improving ability to accurately forecast impending sales. Missed most of forecasted sales in month listed on forecast report, although most eventually closed	2
E. Professionally, efficiently, and respectfully use all of the selling resources provided by the company	• Maintained an excellent relationship with our installation department • Effectively pulled in the engineering department to help close the sale on the Johnson, Smith, Ohio, and Harding accounts • Kept in touch on a regular basis with all the necessary internal departments of our company	4
F. Identify and maintain a positive customer satisfaction level in all assigned accounts	• Maintained a good customer relationship in all accounts for the year except for the Phillips and Harding accounts, which still need more work and effort to improve	2

G. *Internal Company Executives* • Use your management team in sales calls when appropriate and beneficial to your selling efforts	• Took sales manager on regular visits to most important accounts • Effectively used company president on the Harding account	2
External Customer Executives • Maintain a minimum of one upper-level manager or executive at every account assigned	• Need to do more high-level selling. Have not developed enough upper-management contacts in assigned accounts. This is a major territory exposure and needs to be significantly improved immediately. A specific plan will be incorporated into the next performance plan.	1

Section 2 overall ranking: 2

Section 3: Territory Management Objectives

H.   Define territory boundaries or account assignments
I.   Define importance of minimizing lost business
J.   Define maximum expense ranges or expectations
K.   Define territory reporting systems and information flows required, including forecasts and report deadlines / Define accurate report expectations
L.   Define expected productivity and efficiency improvements
M.   Minimize levels of outstanding accounts receivable

Plan	Results Achieved	Ranking
H. Effectively manage and cover all assigned accounts on *19XX Assigned Territory Report,* assigning the appropriate amount of time to meet and exceed quota	• Exceeded assigned quota; however, did not effectively cover all assigned accounts, causing two competitive losses that were both surprises. This problem needs to be corrected and improved, and a specific action plan will be developed for the next performance plan.	1
I. Minimize lost business to competition	• See point H for concern and actions to be taken next year	1
J. Stay within all assigned expense budgets for the year: $15,000 travel budget $7,000 car expense allowance $5,000 car phone and long-distance allowance $10,000 entertainment expense allowance $37,000 Total expense budget	Completed year as follows: $13,000 travel budget $8,000 car expense allowance $7,000 car phone and long-distance allowance $11,000 entertainment expense allowance $39,000 Total expense budget (105% of budget) • Overall, a good job of managing expenses but would prefer staying under budget in future	2

K. All reports will be typed, clear, concise, accurate, and submitted on time. All expense reports will be for reasonable and actual expenses with receipts for all items over $25.00	• Overall a good job; however, sales forecast accuracy needs to be improved (see point D).	2
L. Work to improve overall selling productivity, time management skills, and file organization	• Did a great job moving to new structured calendar system. Seem to be better organized. Keep up the good work; you can still improve this area a lot!	3
M. Maintain a minimum of 5% or less of past due accounts receivable; will stay involved in all collection activities and will ensure that all invoices are collected and not required to be written off as bad debts	• Successfully met all expectations. Good job!	4

Section 3 overall ranking: 2

Section 4: Customer Satisfaction Objectives

N. Define minimum customer service standards
O. Identify need for quick customer problem identification and positive resolution
P. Identify importance of keeping your management team informed and updated on all significant account problems

Plan	Results Achieved	Ranking
N. Ensure that all assigned accounts receive a minimum of four personal on-site sales calls per year (a minimum of one per quarter). Ensure that manager (or higher) visits every account a minimum of once a year and a technical person visits a minimum of twice a year (a minimum of one visit every six months).	• Overall, a fairly good job with larger accounts, but several smaller accounts were ignored. Providing more attention to these important, though smaller, accounts might have prevented loss of accounts to the competition. An action plan needs to be worked on to correct this problem with smaller accounts. (See point H.)	1
O. Ensure that all customer inquiries and/or problems are proactively handled and positively resolved as soon as possible.	• Overall, a good job. Worked hard responding fast to the majority of customer inquiries.	3
P. Keep your manager informed of all potential customer problems. Keep all other relevant departments involved, informed, and updated, as needed	• Good job in this area. Kept me up to date on all situations. • Checked phone messages on a regular basis. • Except for those account loss surprises, everything was kept under control and everyone was informed.	2

Section 4 overall ranking: 2

Section 5: Personal and Professional Development Objectives

Q. Stress importance of being a team player, positive role model, and professional representative of your company

R. Identify personal areas to be developed and education plans to facilitate them (Specify skills in the areas of selling, communication, time management, product knowledge, and industry and business knowledge.)

S. Identify expectations of honesty, ethical behavior, and integrity at all times

Plan	Results Achieved	Ranking
Q. Be a positive and professional team player. Work to be a positive role model for the newer salespeople and at all times be a professional representative of our company and industry	• High energy and positive attitude are a real contribution to our company • Extra efforts to newer people are appreciated	4
R. Develop a personal education plan to improve: • Time and organizational skills • Personal selling skills • X120 and X100 technical product skills and awareness • At least one other skill area to be identified during the year	• Successfully completed the structured calendar system one-day seminar and showed improvement in this area • Listened to three different sales training audio programs • Was scheduled but had to miss technical training due to urgent customer situations. Rescheduled for 2/14/XX. • Attended a sales negotiation program on 5/10/XX	2
S. Always maintain and communicate the highest levels of personal and company honesty and integrity. Always conduct yourself and your actions in a highly ethical and professional manner.	• Good job. Keep up the good work in this area.	4

Section 5 overall ranking: 3

Section 6: Additional Plans and Responsibilities

T.   Identify other behaviors skills, or actions to be worked on
U.   Identify longer-term plans and goals for career development and promotion

Plan	Results Achieved	Ranking
T. This year, work on speaking up when pressured by co-workers and customers. Also work on customer negotiation skills and not giving in as easily when pressured for concessions.	• Improving in this but needs to continue to work on this area of much-needed improvement. Trying hard but still seem to give in to pressure too easily. This is a difficult skill to improve. Your efforts to improve in this area are appreciated.	2
U. Work to pursue goals of being recognized by peers as one of the top salespeople. Also work to expand skills and experiences to move toward the future sales management/goal desired	• Continued growth and sales achievements point toward longer-term personal goals. Keep up the good work!	2

Section 6 overall ranking: 2

Summary

Jane,

You are a high-energy, hard-working sales professional. You are a positive, fun person to work with and are consistently open to suggestions and coaching.

You had a good year coming in at over 100% of your quota for the third year in a row. You have great coverage of your larger accounts, are doing a great job selling new customers, and are an effective communicator both in-house and to your customers.

We need to work this next year on your higher-level management calling skills, your time management skills, your small account coverage, and your ability to handle pressure from coworkers and customers. I am confident you will continue your improvement in these areas — we will develop some specific action plans to include in next year's performance plan.

You are a valuable member of our company and are making a significant contribution to its growth and success. You have a great future in sales — and eventually sales management — as you continue your growth.

Keep up the hard work and extra effort; you have proven that areas you identify for improvement can show results. I am committed to helping you achieve your numbers, as well as your short- and long-term goals.

Keep up the great efforts.

Joe Manager

OVERALL RATING: 3

EXHIBIT 7.3 PERFORMANCE PLAN RATING SCALES

The ratings scales listed here are commonly used by large corporate performance plan programs. The three-point scale is a simpler system; the five-point scale provides the opportunity for more input and coaching direction.

Three-Point Scale

3 = Exceeds job requirements

2 = Meets job requirements

1 = Does not meet job requirements; probation plan identified

Five-Point Scale

5 = Far exceeds job requirements

4 = Consistently exceeds job requirements

3 = Exceeds job requirements in some areas; meets job requirements in others

2 = Meets job requirements

1 = Does not meet job requirements; probation plan identified

CHAPTER 8

MANAGING INFORMATION AND PAPERWORK

So far, we have discussed how to improve your formal and informal communication flows, but *managing* your total information flows involves a lot more written material. Dealing with these flows can become an overwhelming and time-consuming flood if you are not careful.

As a sales manager, you probably spend a phenomenal amount of your time shuffling paper and information. To enhance your overall sales management skills and your ability to effectively communicate with your people, you first need to evaluate the types of information flows you currently use to manage your sales force. When you communicate with one of your sales representatives, what type of information do you tend to focus on?

There are three distinct levels of information flows you see on a daily basis.

1. **History-focused information** includes your salespeople's expense and call reports. With this type of information, the action has already occurred. When dealing with this type of information, make sure you find out exactly what happened and assess the positive or negative aspects of the incident.

2. **Today-focused information** includes your team's status reports and call planning meetings. Problem-resolution activities and customer sales calls are also components of this type of information. Today-focused data tend to require immediate action and implementation. Short-term coordination or planning may also be involved. Some people define their response to today-focused information as "fire fighting" or "crisis management" time.

3. **Future-focused information** includes sales forecasts, quota assignments, employee performance plans, and any account or territory strategic planning. This information deals with long-term strategic, or big-picture, issues. Future-focused discussions usually seek answers to the following questions:

a. How will we make our quota for the year?

b. How will we position our strategic message and uniqueness with that major account?

c. What new markets do we want to focus our attentions on?

d. How do we plan to approach prospects to sell our products/services?

e. How do we plan to get to the right executives to position our company and solutions?

A sales manager needs to include all three levels of information in his or her management efforts. How much time do you spend each week working on these areas? If you are like many sales managers, you are spending about half your time on history-focused information, half on today-focused crisis management, and none at all on future-focused issues. As managers, we get so caught up in finding out what happened and trying to solve this week's crises, there never seems to be any time left for strategic, future-focused discussions.

It is as though we are riding in a car with a salesperson and trying to tell him or her where to go. The front windshield is blacked out, so the only way we can help is to look out the rear window to see what we have already hit or to hang out the side window to see what is preventing us from moving. How can you supply coaching and guidance if you never spend any time looking out the front window?

The issue of future-focused information management becomes especially important when we consider where your people are right now with their information flows. Think about your salespeople's information management skills. Where do they spend their time and energies? Most spend all of their time dealing only with today- and history-focused issues; they have no future focus to any of their selling activities.

Consider testing your team on their future focus. Ask each salesperson what he or she plans to accomplish on the next sales call to his or her best account. Let the person talk as long as he or she wants, but write down the major points he or she wishes to accomplish. Most will talk for at least 10 to 15 minutes and will give you over a dozen goals. When the person is done, ask what he or she plans to accomplish on the second call to this account. The majority of salespeople will say, "Whatever I don't finish from my first call list." Ask what he or she plans to accomplish on the third call to this important account. Ninety percent of all salespeople never think beyond their next customer call, and most do not even think about that call until they are sitting in the customer's parking lot.

Your job as a sales manager is to help each of your people achieve more than they would if left alone. Your people will achieve and sell more if you help them increase their future focus view of their entire territory and their multiple call plans for each of their customers.

As a sales manager, you will need to make three significant changes to your daily information handling if you want to become more balanced with your history-, today-, and future-focused information management. The first is to increase the accuracy of the information itself. The second is to redefine and reevaluate your current information flows and eliminate all ineffective reporting. The third change is to increase the amount of future-focused information you regularly work with.

IMPROVING INFORMATION ACCURACY

To increase your managerial effectiveness, concentrate on increasing the accuracy of information you currently receive from and supply to your sales team. How does information flow within your organization? Most sales teams communicate through a simple, highly ineffective, three-step process:

1. Management demands information from the sales force.
2. The sales team collects and provides the requested information, investing little time and effort.
3. Management uses the data without giving the sales force feedback about report accuracy or why the information was needed.

An overall problem is that the majority of information requested in this way tends to be history- or today-focused and provides little insight into what will help increase sales or profits. Specifically, it is amazing how much information sales representatives assemble when they have absolutely no idea what is being done with it. Sales forecasts and call reports are prime examples of the continual implementation of this flawed three-step system.

Forecasts

How accurate are your team's forecasts? Are your salespeople aware of what you and your management team do with the forecasts they turn in?

Consider the following situation. A manufacturer of printing inks and food coloring additives had a serious problem with its sales team's forecasting efforts. The company sold over 100 different products nationally, and manufacturing was done at a single complex. The majority of products were produced for immediate sale; few products were manufactured for general inventory. This made the accuracy of each month's manufacturing schedule of prime importance. Fifteen salespeople worked out of their homes across the country and reported to one sales manager, who spent over half his time selling to his own accounts. The representatives' monthly sales forecasts were consistently inaccurate. Management felt the problem was the representatives' lack of forecasting skills, but the real problem was that the management team was using the ineffective three-step communication process to request information. The management team summarized the monthly sales forecasts submitted by each salesperson into a single report. Production management then set the plant's manufacturing schedule according to this report. Because of the inaccuracy of the individual sales forecasts, production often did not meet customer demand, or the company was left with old inventory.

So what was the problem? It turned out that management had never told the sales force what it was doing with the completed forecasts. The salespeople complained for years because they saw the reports purely as a management exercise that had no value to them and no relevance to the rest of the company. Because of this and the fact that they were never given feedback on their forecasting accuracy or on how the reports were used, they put almost no effort into preparing them. Although they knew their reporting was inaccurate, they did not feel this was a serious problem because no one in management had ever complained to them. For this manufacturer, the issue was not a lack of forecasting skills, but a lack of communication between the sales team and management.

To increase the accuracy and relevance of the information you receive from your sales team, try the following steps:

1. Compare last year's monthly forecasts to what was actually sold each month. Some companies using this method have found their accuracy rating to be as low as 10 percent to 20 percent. If these numbers are similar to yours, over 80 percent of your team's monthly forecasts may be completely inaccurate.

2. Make your salespeople accountable for the information they provide. At the end of each month, give each salesperson a copy of his or her last forecast showing what actually happened, and give a percentage score, or grade, on the accuracy of the report.

3. Keep track of the scores and invest some coaching time with each of your people to discuss ways to improve the forecasts. Just knowing you are keeping score can generate an immediate improvement.

4. Take time to help team members identify long-term selling strategies for each of their important accounts. The more future-focused planning your salespeople do, the more accurate their forecasts will be.

Call Reports

Although monthly sales forecasts are a major problem in many organizations, an even greater one may be posed by the weekly call reports submitted by the sales force. Kathleen, a vice president of sales at an ice cream manufacturer, had each of her people submit the normal weekly call reports outlining who he or she had called on for the week and what had been accomplished. To enhance the accuracy of the reports and to increase her coaching efforts, she went through each call report every week and marked them up with a red pen. She wrote notes of congratulations, sales ideas, or suggestions for specific account promotions. Since the call reports were two-part forms, she sent the top copy back to the representative, and the bottom copy was placed in his or her file. Whenever Kathleen rode with a salesperson, she would bring the salesperson's call report file along, ask questions, and discuss the last few months' reports. She believed, "It's much harder to fake it when you know your manager's watching and commenting on everything you submit in your call reports."

How do you feel about taking the time each week to mark up all your salespeople's call reports? Most sales managers say they do not have enough time to invest in such a time-consuming effort. If this is true for you too, then why are you requesting such extensive materials from each of your salespeople that take up so much of their time? The majority of call reports ask for far too much detail on issues and areas that will not have a direct impact on increasing the sales of your team. The more information you request from your people without any ongoing feedback, the less accurate the information will be.

Look at it from the salesperson's perspective. As a salesperson, you are expected to submit detailed weekly call reports and extensive monthly sales forecasts. You have dutifully turned in all your reports on time for the last several months. Each weekly call report takes over an hour to prepare, and your monthly sales forecast takes over two hours. For the past year, you have heard nothing from management about the quality or the accuracy of any of your reports; no one even mentions these reports once they are turned in. The only management concern seems to be that you submit your reports on time. If this happened to you, how much time would you invest in this week's call report? Is it possible that you might not spend as much time or generate as accurate a report as you have in the past? What is the risk of increasing your efficiency and time management by investing less in these reports? There are some salespeople who would slack off on the reports and wait to see if their managers notice any difference. If their managers complain, they return to the previous, more accurate, method of preparing their reports. But if their managers say nothing, it proves to them that they were justified in improving their time efficiency and reducing their report accuracy. What type of message have you communicated to your sales team over the last year?

Take a look at your last few months of call reports. Is all of the information really critical to your team's success? If no one is reading it, why are you asking for so much material in the first place? Call reports are meant to be a positive information source to help keep the management team informed on the direction and efforts of the sales force. They are not meant to be a "policing" document to prove your salespeople are actually working. Call reports are too easily "faked" or enhanced to look like a salesperson has been working hard all week. The reality is that the vast majority of salespeople have, at some time, listed imaginary calls or conversations on their call reports to make it look like they put in more effort than they actually did.

What else can you do to increase the accuracy of the information your salespeople submit to you?

- Review all the types of information currently being collected by your sales team. Decide what information is critical and identify what information is not significantly contributing to your team's selling efforts and success.

- Change your mix of communicating history-, today-, and future-focused information with your sales team. Your people will follow your example. What can you do to change your behaviors and actions so your people get the message they also need to change their mix of communications?

- Discuss what your salespeople can do to increase the accuracy of the information they report, and the ways they can increase report preparation efficiency. It is critical for you to communicate how their information is being used and viewed within the company. How much time do you spend reviewing their reports? How much of your evaluation of job performances and salary raises are based on the timeliness and accuracy of your sales team's weekly and monthly reports?

- Share with your people how other managers, including senior managers, perceive their reports. How do these reports help to influence the leadership and direction of your company? How do these reports reflect on the professionalism and skill of the sales team?

- Let your sales team know how this information can benefit their territory management efforts. Be sure your people understand how they can use these reports in their own territory planning on an ongoing basis. Also, discuss how these reports can be used to produce more of a future focus to their sales efforts (this is discussed later in the chapter).

- Review with upper management the types of information your sales-people are currently collecting. How much of this information is unnecessary, redundant, or simply not worth the time and effort it is taking to collect? Push your managers to understand that the more information requested, the greater the likelihood that overall information accuracy will decline. Point out that every hour invested in information collection is an hour removed from available selling time.

- For the next few months, discuss all reports with your salespeople when they submit them to you. How much time did it take for them to complete the report? How accurate do they feel the report is? What did they change from their last report that will help improve its accuracy?

- What can they do to add more of a future focus to this information? How are other managers benefiting from this information?

The idea is to reinventory all of the information requests you make of your salespeople. Make sure they fully understand what happens to their reports after they are turned in. Every several months, make sure you go over, in detail, how their reports and information are processed and used by the rest of the organization and discuss how inaccurate data can have a negative overall effect. Finally, evaluate how you, as their manager, can increase your specific feedback on the accuracy and helpfulness of the information they provide.

REDEFINING INFORMATION FLOWS

You now need to redefine and re-evaluate all the sales information flows and reports generated by you, your company, and your sales force. Consider how your current reporting levels and forms came about. The majority of information demands evolve over time. What may have started as a simple, one-page weekly activity report can, over months or years, easily grow into a multiple-page weekly call report. How have your information flows and reports evolved over time?

Part of your responsibility as a sales manager is to guard your sales team from extraneous information requests from the rest of the company. How many requests for time-consuming, yet ultimately unimportant reports have you seen other departments ask for? Others most likely do not understand the pressures and responsibilities of selling and may actually feel that sales reps have lots of extra time or are not working very hard anyway. How do you screen the information requests for your team? Do you evaluate every request to see if it will help or enhance your selling efforts?

For example, consider the trust department of a large bank that brought in a new manager named Tom to take responsibility for all trust investments. Tom immediately instituted a rule that every computer printout, report, and request for information had to go through him before any action could be taken. He discovered that 10-pound computer printouts were being generated monthly, but no one ever looked at them. He also learned that other departments were requesting activity reports that did nothing to increase the competitiveness or quality of his people's investment work. In his first 60 days on the job, Tom reduced annual internal computer charges by over $150,000. He completely revised the antiquated information flows that had been in place for years. Tom said he needed to clean up the department's information flows before he could begin improving his people's investment efforts and abilities.

How much useless paper and information does your company generate? Are other departments using the information your sales team is giving them? For instance, how important is it that marketing personnel receive a detailed breakdown of each customer's brochure usage? Is there a more efficient way to collect information the engineering department says it needs on customer ordering procedures?

Instead of blindly accepting the next new information requests, consider evaluating the time investment and lost sales required for your salespeople to properly collect, prepare, and report on the required data. Fight useless information requests. Ask whoever generated the request to prove how the information will actually help you become:

- more focused in selling and marketing,
- more productive and efficient,
- more competitive and unique,
- more aware of activity in your territories, or
- more aware of what you need to sell.

If the person cannot relate the information's importance to these goals, refuse the request. Also, consider reviewing all existing information requests within your company to make sure they are valid. If you work in a large company with many sales managers, be sure to get the support of your manager as well as that of your fellow sales managers.

INCREASING YOUR FUTURE FOCUS

The third and final change that can enhance your information flows is to increase the future focus of you and your sales team. One of the easiest and most effective ways to do this is to significantly change how and what information is collected on your weekly call reports. These reports are arguably the most overused, ineffective management tools available to sales managers. Let us look at the problems with these reports and then discuss ways they can be improved.

Call Report Problems and Solutions

Complexity. The first problem with call reports is that they have evolved over the years into detailed, complex reports that ask for far too much information. They may have started out as simple documents, but about once a year someone added a new column or line of information to be collected. Some companies require salespeople to give the length of time required for a call, a detailed listing of what promotional materials were passed out, and whether they walked through the customer's plant. What does a management team do with this data? Look at the call reports your people fill out and determine which information is critical to your ability to effectively manage and coach your salespeople.

Lack of Feedback. The second major problem with most call reports is the lack of feedback to the salespeople generating them. You demand volumes of complex information from your team and then give no feedback or even prove you are reading the reports. Why would representatives be concerned with the validity of their reporting if they believe their manager does not review their work? It is not uncommon for salespeople to sit on airplanes or in restaurants on Friday afternoons filling out their weekly call reports. Some even prepare their reports without opening their calendars. If you expect these reports to be accurate, you have to provide feedback to your salespeople.

Inaccuracy. The third major problem of call reports is their inaccuracy. The majority of salespeople see a call report as something management demands but with little personal value. For most experienced representatives, call reports become more of a way to tell managers what they want to hear than a factual report of what really happened during the week. Think back to when you were in sales. Did you ever look at your completed call report and think, this is not enough work to impress my boss or my company? What did you do? If you were like most salespeople, you became creative and prepared a great report that showed how hard you had worked that week. You were confident your sales manager was too overworked and busy to look at the report closely. Sales team members at one company privately refer to their weekly call reports as "Disney" reports. The joke is that if their managers believe the accuracy of the reports, they also believe that Mickey Mouse is really a 500-pound rodent who works at the park. How much accuracy and effort are your salespeople putting into their call reports? Prove to your salespeople that you actually review their reports, and accuracy will improve.

History Focused. The fourth problem with call reports is that all the information collected is completely history focused. It is the classic example we discussed earlier about trying to steer a car without looking forward. Suppose you receive a weekly call report showing where a salesperson has supposedly been and on whom he or she has called. What can you do with this information? Everything on that report is history. As a sales manager and a coach, you now can react only to actions that have already occurred or mistakes that have already been made. Instead of working with historical information, ask your people to fill out their call reports in advance, listing where they plan to be during the coming week.

You can easily convert your existing, relatively useless, history-focused reports into future-focused, productive management coaching tools. You will still ask for the same types of information, but ask for it *before* the work is completed. When would you rather help your team members — prior to a call, when you can have a positive influence, or after the call, when you can only react and complain?

To implement future-focused weekly call reports, make up new forms that divide the existing call report into three columns, as illustrated in Exhibit 8.1. The first column identifies the day of the week the call will take place; the second column identifies the company, contact name, and contact's title; the next column lists the salesperson's plans for each call for the next week; and the last column states what actually took place. At the beginning of the week, ask all salespeople to submit their new call reports with the first three columns filled out. This way, you can talk to them and offer advice before they make their sales calls. You can also coach them on how to effectively maximize their work efforts for the week. At the end of the week, ask your people to give you a copy of the reports with the last column filled in. They need to also list comments about additional unplanned or last-minute conversations or scheduled calls that occurred and submit their plans for the following week.

If you decide to change from a history-focused format to a blended past and future reporting system, consider exactly what information you need from your sales force. Too many businesses complicate call reports. They are not meant to be a complete customer history; they are only intended to help you, as the sales manager, understand what is happening in all of the sales territories. As you reexamine your reporting system, determine how you can increase your coaching and feedback to your salespeople. One of the best ways to ensure the accuracy of any report is to continually prove your interest in the information collected.

SUMMARY

As a successful sales manager, you need to increase the efficiency, accuracy, and quality of the information your sales team generates. The better your information, the higher the quality of the motivational environment you can help your people create. You also need to reduce or eliminate unnecessary paperwork to create time for strategic skill development. The less time you and your salespeople need to handle the operational, today-focused details, the more time you can spend on long-term, strategic, future-focused business planning. Even your paperwork can be revised to focus on future opportunities rather than on past actions. This emphasis on improving the motivational environment of your team by honing your strategic focus is examined more thoroughly in the next chapter.

EXHIBIT 8.1 FUTURE-FOCUSED CALL REPORT FORM

WEEKLY CALL REPORT

Name _____

Division _____

Week of _____

Day of Week	Company/Contact Person/Title	Plans and Goals for Sales Call	Actual Results from Sales Call

CHAPTER 9

STRENGTHENING YOUR STRATEGIC FOCUS

Throughout this book, we have explored the two most critical responsibilities you have as a sales manager: managing your sales team and the selling process. Most of our discussion has focused on your people management skills. Enhancing your leadership, training, and coaching skills improves your ability to manage the sales process.

Successfully managing the selling process requires you to maximize your sales management skills in three distinct areas of responsibility, illustrated in Exhibit 9.1:

- Working to ensure your selling environment is strategically focused to help your people improve their message of competitive uniqueness.
- Maximizing your sales management leadership, training, and coaching skills.
- Helping your salespeople increase their strategic vision.

We will devote the next three chapters to a detailed examination of each of these responsibilities.

INCREASING YOUR ENVIRONMENT'S STRATEGIC FOCUS

Your first area of responsibility is to make sure your selling environment is strategically focused to help your salespeople increase their message of competitive uniqueness. How much control and input do you have toward the strategic leadership of your company? Some sales managers have more flexibility than others in changing their selling message and focus. No matter how flexible or rigid your company, you still need to make sure your selling environment is correctly focused, and that your entire team has a strong sense of your company's message of competitive uniqueness and how to deliver that message successfully to all customers and prospects.

One way to accomplish this is to strengthen and clarify your company's strategic direction by guiding your management team through a three-step process designed to increase its competitive uniqueness:

1. Clarify your corporate position and selling strategy in your market, and identify the customers and prospects you want your salespeople to sell and support.

2. Redefine your competitive uniqueness message and focus in your market.

3. Refocus your salespeople so their sales efforts reinforce your competitive message of uniqueness and help achieve company goals. Ensure that all of your people consistently and persuasively deliver this message to all prospects and customers.

CLARIFYING YOUR POSITION AND SELLING STRATEGY

There are most likely many direct competitors your customers could buy from. In today's intensely competitive environment, your competitors have proven they can do a good job and can satisfy the same customers if given a chance. A high-quality product or service that was competitively priced and backed with a strong level of support used to be enough of a competitive advantage to get customers to buy from you and remain loyal. But, in today's tougher marketplace, just doing a good job is no longer enough. Today, we all face strong competitors bidding for the same business. Why, based on all the competitive alternatives, would a buyer select you?

Ask your sales team this question. Most salespeople cannot answer it effectively. The majority of salespeople are effective at answering the question "Why would I want to buy from you?" Answering in a vacuum, assuming you have no competitive concerns is easy, but what do you say when your competitors are also being considered and they too can do a good job for the customer? The following section includes a test you can give your team that demonstrates the importance of using the three-step process to answer "Why, based on all of the competitive alternatives available to me, would I want to buy from you?" Successfully answering this question can help your team increase your strategic focus and competitive advantage.

Salespeople's Perspective

Ask at least three of your salespeople what they think is unique about your company and its products or services. What do they say to get customers to buy from them instead of the competition? Use their answers to build an inventory of the major features and concepts they use to communicate your competitive uniqueness. Write the answers on a wall board or flip chart so everyone can see them. Make sure to keep your list on the left side of the available space. When you have at least ten items, draw a vertical line down the center of the page and write the name of your toughest competitor at the top of the right side.

Now ask your team to specify what this competitor is currently telling customers that makes them unique in your market. Remind your people that reality means nothing here. All that matters is the customer's *perception* of reality. It does not matter if your product is of higher quality than your competitor's or that the competitor is making the same high-quality claims — the customer cannot tell the difference. When both lists are complete, your people can see that you are most likely giving the same message to your customers as your competition is.

Customer Perceptions

At the same time you are researching your team's perceptions of your competitive message of uniqueness, you also need to research your existing customer base. What are the real reasons your customers are saying they buy from you? What do they see as your competitive advantages or unique strengths? It would also help to interview several of your competitor's best customers to better understand why they buy from them. It takes persuasive, probing questions to get the answers you need. Consider using a form like the customer telephone outline questionnaire shown in Exhibit 9.2 to record your findings and to keep everyone's focus the same. Your salespeople can help with this research, but be aware that the interviewing will be done best if you handle it personally.

It is advisable to conduct this kind of customer survey on a regular basis. Each month, select several customers to call and interview. Face-to-face interviews will give you the most useful answers but you may also use the telephone. Do *not* use a form letter. Several studies have shown that this type of customer research does not provide clear, useful information. The only customers who tend to fill out written surveys are those who are either happy with their sales representative and want to help him or her look good, or those who are angry and are looking for a way to vent their frustrations. Customers who are merely satisfied or are nearing a frustration level are not likely to respond in writing. A personal meeting may be worth the extra effort to find out how they really feel about your company.

Consider calling any customer who places a large order with your company. You, as the sales manager, can call to thank him or her for selecting your company. This is a great lead-in to asking some big-picture questions about how and why the customer selected you. It also allows you to ask about your competitors' messages and what your company could have done better to have made the customer's decision even easier. For your larger customers, you may want to repeat this interview every six months or annually. It is acceptable to have your salespeople ask these questions of your normal- to smaller-sized customers at least annually. An outline of your interview with "new" customers could include:

1. I wanted to call as the manager responsible for your business to personally thank you for selecting our company and to reaffirm that [salesperson's name], our entire company, and I are committed to going the "extra mile" to ensure you long-term satisfaction with the quality and support of our products/services.

2. Your business is important to us and we want to make sure we are able to fulfill your expectations of why you selected us. To ensure that we do a consistently high-quality job for you, help me understand why, based on all of the competitive alternatives available, you selected our company.

   a. What did you like best about what we do compared to the other choices you had?

   b. What, no matter how small or insignificant, would you have liked to have seen us do better that would have made your choice even easier?

   c. What did you like most about our competitors that you wish we did or offered more of?

3. May I check back with you on a regular basis to make sure we continue to provide you with the quality and support you expect? Your business is important to all of us at [your company name]. [Salesperson's name] will be responsible for getting you the information and support you need to successfully use our products/services. If he/she is not available, or you are not satisfied with our responses for any reason, please give me a call.

Interviewing Your Competitive Losses

Asking your competitive losses these questions can also give you some critical insight into your competition and why you lost the account. An outline of a suggested interview with "lost" buyers might include:

1. I wanted to call as the manager responsible for your business to personally thank you for considering our company. All of us at [your company name] regret that you chose not to select our proposal. We worked hard to communicate the reasons we feel we have a superior product/service. It is evident that either we didn't do our homework about your business or we didn't do a good enough job communicating why we could do the best job for your company.

2. We regret, but accept, your decision to buy from [your competitor's name]. They are a good company and will do a good job for you. (*Note*: You have to say your competitor is a good company and will do a good job, even if you feel it is untrue. If you say anything negative or neutral about your competition at this point, you will insult the buyer and lose the chance of getting the information you want. This buyer thinks your competition can do a better job than you. That is why he or she chose them. If you imply that the buyer is stupid for selecting the competition, you will get only defensive answers that will have no value to you.)

3. We would like the opportunity to try again in the future to re-earn your business and your trust. May I ask some questions to better

understand what we need to correct or improve to help us be more competitive in the future?

4. [Competitor's name] is a good company. Why, based on all of the competitive alternatives available to you, did you select them?

   a. What did you like best about what they do compared to our company and the other competitive choices you had?

   b. What do you see as our greatest negative or weakness?

   c. What would you like to have seen us do better that would have made us more competitive?

   d. What would you have liked to see [competitor's name] do that would have made them even easier to select?

5. We thank you again for considering us. May [your salesperson's name] check back with you periodically to see if we can work to earn your business in the future?

Be aware that when interviewing a buyer that chose your competition they may not want to answer too many questions. The goal is to interview as many competitive losses as possible so that their answers can help you gain information and insight into your competitors' selling messages. Also be aware that your attitude during these interviews is critical to the openness and quality of the responses you receive. You will close all discussion if you show any sign of skepticism or try to defend your company or argue with what the customer believes is true. Remember the buyer chose the other company because, somehow, you and your company didn't get your message across clear enough to satisfy his or her requirements. Reality means nothing. All that matters is the customer's perception of reality.

Buyers Who Cite Price for Their Decision. No matter what you sell, no customer has ever used price as their primary decision factor. At most, price is the second most important factor the buyer considers. The most important factor is always the differential in value offered by the various competitors. If the buyer sees a significantly positive differential in one company's value, that company will get the business. Only if the buyer sees little or no difference in value between several companies will he or she then make a selection based on price. After all, what is a "commodity" except a product that buyers view as having no value differential no matter who they buy it from. What is the job of a salesperson except to work to maximize the proof of value differential compared to the competition? A simple selling formula is that the more of a competitive difference you can prove regarding your value, the more of a competitive difference you can achieve in price. The salesperson's job is to prove that your company has a positive value differential to the buyer. If the buyer ignores or does not see this differential and buys based on price, your salesperson did not do his or her primary job with that customer. It is critical that you, as a sales manager, communicate this "value-to-price differential" concept to all your salespeople. Otherwise, they will rationalize any competitive loss to you by saying, "It wasn't my fault because they bought based only on price."

When conducting your competitive loss interviews, never accept "the competitor's price was lower" as a final answer. If the buyer uses this response, consider asking the following questions:

- We appreciate that [competitor's name] offered you a lower price to win your business. All of us in this industry are working on smaller margins in today's tougher marketplace. How did they prove to you they could deliver the same level of quality and service than your other choices even though they were going to be supporting you on much smaller margins?

- How did they prove you were not taking a significantly greater risk by accepting their lower price?

- How did they make you comfortable that you were not going to get a lower level of support of quality?

In all of your competitive loss interviews, the buyer will most likely not answer all your questions. But calling all losses to try to learn something from each can help you learn more about your competition and improve your sales team's effectiveness in delivering your competitive selling message. How many competitive losses in the past year have you personally talked to about why they bought from someone else?

Planning for Change

Once you have some customer feedback, the next step is to conduct strategic planning sessions. Set aside at least two full days for these sessions, and hold them off-site to minimize interruptions. If you are a smaller company, be sure to include all your company's top executives and your senior salespeople. If you are part of a large corporation, you will want to get the top executives of your division involved. Some type of executive buy-in and support is critical to this (and future) step.

The purpose of these meetings is to redefine and clarify your message of competitive uniqueness and your proactive selling strategic focus. You also want to target changes that will refocus and clarify your company's selling direction and competitive advantage. To help redefine your strategic focus, ask your management team the following questions:

1. What business are we really in?
2. Why are our best customers really buying from us?
3. What markets or customer niches do we want our company to grow over the next five years?
4. What is our competitive advantage?
5. How are we competitively positioned?
6. With which customers do we have the greatest competitive advantage?

The first two questions clarify your present market position. As long as your customers have a competitive choice, they are not buying from you because of your specific products or services; they are buying your ability to deliver something different and special. What are your customers really buying from you? You may sell computers, but your customer is actually buying the ability to enhance his or her business information flows. Question 3 looks at future growth and opportunities, while questions 4, 5, and 6 stimulate discussion about how to achieve that growth. Once you have answered these questions, determine the actions necessary to increase your competitive market advantage.

Redefining and clarifying your corporate position and selling strategy is a major managerial undertaking. It can be tiring and difficult, but when conducted properly, these off-site discussions can be well worth the investment.

REDEFINING YOUR COMPETITIVE UNIQUENESS

Once you have clarified your strategic corporate position and market selling strategy, the second step in increasing your competitive advantage is to redefine your competitive uniqueness.

Look back at the first list your sales team generated that identified why you and your competitors are unique. Is your message to your customers any different than your competitor's message? As we've said, the answer is usually no. Communicating your competitive uniqueness means your salespeople need to present a *consistent* message that is more customer-focused than the competition's.

Establishing a Common Message

To redefine your competitive uniqueness, you need to continue your customer research and identify the full range of messages currently being delivered by your sales force. It is common for five salespeople working in the same office to deliver five completely different messages to their customers and prospects. One representative might focus on your company's years in the business; another may stress your delivery commitments; and a third might base persuasion on your price advantage.

Your goal is to see that all your people spread the same message of uniqueness so your customers understand your selling strategy. If you are not consistently reviewing and restating your message with your sales team on at least a monthly basis, you can expect each person to deliver a different version of your company's message.

One company that produced water processing equipment found that each of its 12 salespeople were communicating different messages of uniqueness to their respective customers. One of the representatives referenced an existing installation to help close another sale. A tour was arranged so the prospect could visit the current installation, but after the tour, the prospect expressed concern. The established customer had tried hard to help the salesperson's efforts by recounting the reasons they did business with this manufacturer: low price and the salesperson's helpfulness. Unfortunately, the prospect had been sold on superior service and equipment support. The sale was eventually saved, but the incident convinced management that a consistent company wide strategic selling message was needed.

After extensive strategic planning and team discussions, the company developed a competitive selling message that everyone was comfortable with. Several test presentations to existing customers and potential prospects proved the uniqueness of this new message, which was not radically different than what some of the sales team had been using. It was now more focused and clarified so the entire team could use it. To make sure the new selling message had become a part of every selling situation, the sales manager asked three salespeople to stand up at different times during each quarterly sales meeting and present the new selling message of uniqueness to the rest of the sales team. This repetition kept the message fresh in everyone's mind and gave them examples of how it could be modified to fit each salesperson's personal selling style.

Focusing on Philosophy

A strong competitive message of uniqueness only enhances your selling efforts. As you work to clarify how and why you are unique in your market, remember that the effectiveness of your message is based on its customer focus. Many salespeople focus only on their products, and their sales presentations incorporate the message, "Our products are better than theirs because . . . " This type of message may no longer be effective due to improvements your competitors may have made over the last several years. How different is your product or service compared to your competition's? How relevant are these differences to your customers? Most car salespeople can list 50 differences between their cars and those of their competitors. But, as a car buyer, how many of those differences are so minor to you that they end up having no impact on your decision to buy a particular car?

You significantly increase your competitive advantage when you can show that you have a different competitive philosophy or approach. The most successful competitive philosophies are those that focus on areas such as lowest risk or highest long-term value. Let us assume you run a business delivery service, and you want Paula, the buyer at Company XYZ, to use your service. There are a number of competitors who offer the same services in your area, so why would she choose you? Instead of talking about your delivery services, try focusing on your selling philosophy by saying,

Paula, you have a wide range of companies to choose from and the majority of them can handle your local same-day deliveries. The differences between our companies are not based on the service offerings, but on our philosophy of supporting your business. Most of the other companies offer you a minimum price combined with a minimum level of service to try to keep your business. Our philosophy is based on a "least risk" approach by working with you and your company. Anyone can offer to deliver your packages, but how much risk are you willing to take with your same-day delivery requirements? We are "least risk" because we offer the largest fleet of trucks in the city. Our large fleet size means we have the best chance of consistently picking up your orders in the minimum amount of time. We are also "least risk" to you because of our extensive and ongoing customer service training for all employees and our certified drug and alcohol testing programs for all our drivers. It won't matter if you saved a few dollars on a package delivery if the driver has too many other pick-ups or has an accident and forces you to miss a deadline or a promised delivery. To help you lower your risk even further, all our trucks are equipped with radios and cellular telephones to let you check on the status of your delivery at any time.

All delivery companies will promise to do a good job delivering your same-day packages. But we want to be the company that talks to you about how we can lower your delivery risk and help you run your business more profitably. Our prices may be a few dollars more, but we can prove that our "least risk" approach can be your lowest total cost of business.

This is the type of selling philosophy message that can help you differentiate your approach from your product-based competitors.

As you clarify your new selling message, you will need to revise the standard sales presentation and brochures your sales team currently uses.

The majority of sales literature is only focused on products and looks almost identical to your competitors' printed materials. Redoing everything at once can be a costly endeavor, but at least some of your literature needs to address and support your competitive message of uniqueness. A good start is to work at changing your customer cover letters to include your new message. Even if you still use your current product-based literature, at least your cover letter can communicate your new philosophy.

Gaining Support

Once you have developed a workable competitive message, the final phase in redefining your competitive uniqueness is gaining company support for making changes to your selling efforts. It is all too common for a sales management team to outline all the ways they can improve their competitive advantage, only to be shot down because no one will agree to spending the money to make the necessary improvements.

Consider making your company's executive management team an integral part of your planning process to ensure they "buy into" your new selling direction. Sell other department heads on the benefits of your new sales direction and ask them to convince their people of the need for everyone to support and communicate these new selling messages. It will not matter what your salespeople say if your drivers, telemarketers, receptionists, and other front-line people contradict your new selling message. The company, as a whole, has to be committed to communicating a stronger competitive position in the market.

REFOCUSING YOUR SALESPEOPLE

Once you have a clear selling vision and a solid message of competitive uniqueness, the third and most difficult step in strategically increasing your competitive advantage is to refocus your salespeople. The first phase of refocusing your salespeople is to reevaluate and redefine their priorities. An important part of your job is to continually discuss with your people what priorities, directions, and actions they need to follow.

One manufacturer of answering machines sold its product through an independent distribution network. The manufacturer's 10-person sales force was responsible for selling to and supporting the distributors. Each of the manufacturer's salespeople was responsible for approximately 100 separate accounts over a multi-state area. The representatives found that the more support they gave their best distributors, the more total product they sold. Each representative consistently generated 80 percent of their total sales from their top 10 distributor accounts. The team was asked to identify how they divided their time and efforts. After some discussion, the representatives determined that they spent about 70 percent of their time prospecting and about 30 percent with their top 10 accounts. Consider how ridiculous these priorities are. Why would salespeople devote only 30 percent of their time to the accounts that generated 80 percent of their revenue? No one ever told them to allocate their time that way — the practice just evolved over time.

How much more could salespeople sell if they spent the majority of their time supporting the top 10 accounts that were generating over 80 percent of their revenue? It has been consistently proven that focusing your time in accordance with your sources of revenue is the easiest way to grow your total revenue. If over 80 percent of your revenue comes from the top 10 percent of your territory, how much more could you sell if you gave these "best" accounts even more support and attention? Why would you want to *under*support your best accounts? Prospecting and efforts to support the rest of your territory are important enough that you may not want to devote a full 80 percent of your time to these top accounts, but what kind of an impact would providing 60 percent or 70 percent of your time have on increasing your sales?

The average salesperson generates over 80 percent of his or her revenue from the top 20 percent of his or her accounts, but only gives these accounts about 30 percent of his or her total time. Salespeople also tend to generate less than 3 percent of their total revenue from the bottom 10 percent of their accounts, but still invest between 8 percent and 12 percent of their time supporting these low-revenue generators. Most territories become unbalanced like this through normal operational evolution. This type of imbalance could have existed for years, since neither the salesperson nor the sales manager had a strong enough strategic awareness to fix such a significant territory management problem. This type of account balance makes sense when it is evaluated in the big-picture view.

How much time have you spent recently discussing your sales team's priorities and selling focus? Regularly ask your people how they focus their selling efforts and consider asking them to calculate the percentage of selling time they spend with each account. How can you coach them to refocus their time allocations to more closely agree with the allocation of their revenues? You also need to improve executive and sales management attention to and support for your sales force. When was the last time you sat down with a salesperson to discuss anything other than today-focused customer emergencies? If you work in a large corporation, when was the last time your executives paid any attention to or spent any time talking

---

TEAM LEADER'S TOOL

HELPING YOUR SALESPEOPLE PRIORITIZE

You need to increase your salesforce's awareness of their activities before you can help them improve their skills. Try the following territory analysis for your representatives:

1. List all their customers from last year along with the revenue each of those accounts generated. List them in descending order so the first customer is the one that spent the most money.

2. Do a cumulative percentage total so you can see how many customers it took to generate the top 10 percent of their total sales for the year. How many of their best customers did it take to generate the top 50 percent of their total sales? (Normally, the bottom 10 percent of sales probably came from over 20 percent of the smallest accounts.)

3. Give your salespeople a list of their accounts in order of sales volume but without the sales figures. Ask them to identify how much time they spend with each of these accounts.

4. After they have assigned percentages to each account, show them the revenue numbers ranked by amount of sales and compare the time invested with the revenues actually generated. Then discuss what they can do to reprioritize their territory time investment to best increase their total sales revenue.

with your team members? As a sales manager, it is your responsibility to make sure executives and other department heads are maintaining a dialogue with your sales force.

One senior executive stays informed of sales progress through memos on any significant activity. Because he is busy with other responsibilities, he has his sales managers write congratulatory notes for him to sales representatives who have put forth extra effort. He then signs the notes. The sales force feels the executive is closely involved, and he stays updated on major selling progress without a serious time investment. This kind of attention can significantly enhance your team's productivity and effectiveness, as well as motivate them to accept new directions in corporate selling strategy.

SUMMARY

To strengthen your company's strategic selling focus, work with your entire sales and management team to develop a sales message that truly communicates your company's uniqueness. Once your new selling message is developed, make sure that everyone in the company makes it a priority to regularly convey that uniqueness to your customers.

This chapter focused on the first skill area you need to improve to successfully manage the selling process: working to ensure your selling environment is strategically focused to help your people increase their message of competitive uniqueness. The next chapter explores how to maximize your sales management leadership, training, and coaching skills.

EXHIBIT 9.1 KEYS TO MANAGING THE SELLING PROCESS

EXHIBIT 9.2 CUSTOMER TELEPHONE OUTLINE QUESTIONNAIRE

Date: _____

Customer: _____

Customer Contact: _____

In this customer's eyes, what makes our company unique?

_____

_____

_____

Why do they buy from us instead of the competition?

_____

_____

_____

What kind of competitive advantage do they think we have?

_____

_____

_____

What are our weaknesses? What exposure could endanger our present or future relationship?

_____

_____

_____

What do we need to do to be more competitive in this market?

_____

_____

_____

Other comments:

_____

_____

_____

Note: You can also use this same outline (with minor wording changes) when calling the competition's customers.

CHAPTER 10

COACHING YOUR SALESPEOPLE

Most sales managers never really coach their people. They offer occasional suggestions and advice, but they rarely help with planning for an important sales call. Coaching a salesperson takes time, but is a worthwhile training experience. To enhance the productivity and effectiveness of your salespeople, you need to be a good coach and a good teacher. In this chapter, you can master the finer points of coaching your team in six different situations:

- Precall planning meeting
- Sales call
- Call debriefing
- "Ride-withs"
- Crises
- Loss of a major account

What style of management do you use in teaching your people? Are you a top gun or a coach? Refer back to our discussion of management styles in Chapter 3, and review the characteristics of each of these managers. Remember the advantages to using a coaching style? This style leads to a "teaching guide" approach to training. The teaching guide sales manager knows that the only lessons we retain are those we learn for ourselves. As a guide, your responsibility is to ask your people questions that force them to evaluate alternatives and outcomes, and eventually find the "right" answers on their own. The more questions you ask, the more effective your coaching will be.

Let us look closely at the six most prevalent situations in which salespeople can benefit from your coaching and training.

PRECALL PLANNING MEETING

The first step of the sales call coaching process is the precall planning meeting. The goal of this meeting is to make sure the sales representative knows exactly what he or she wants to accomplish. Is he or she aware of the various directions the call may take? Has he or she decided what the next selling step after this call will be? To help the salesperson focus on these issues, ask him or her the following questions:

- Why are you making this sales call?
- What do you hope to accomplish?
- What is the customer's personality? How will you modify your selling approach to parallel the customer's personality and increase your personal persuasiveness?
- What questions can you ask to learn something new about their business, their buying environment, or your competition's activities?
- What "road blocks" or problems might come up during your call?
- How will you handle the call if the customer says . . . ?

If you are working with a new sales representative, you may want to ask about what they plan to say during each of the structured steps of a sales call. If you are going along on the call, you also need to ask if the customer is expecting you, what role the salesperson would like you to play on the call, and what sign he or she will give if your help is required during the call.

This precall planning meeting may take only 15 minutes with an experienced salesperson or two hours with a newer representative. Effective precall planning is done in the quiet of your office, over the telephone, or during the long drive to a customer's office. Most sales managers make the mistake of asking precall coaching questions as they approach the customer's front door or when they are waiting in the lobby. Three minutes immediately before the call is not enough time to ask all the necessary questions or to give your salesperson a chance to think through the alternatives.

THE SALES CALL

How and when is it best for a sales manager to accompany a salesperson on a sales call? Effective precall planning and coaching reduces the need for you to go on sales calls, but a lot of managers feel this is one of their most important job functions.

The Manager's Purpose on a Sales Call

If you are working with someone who has never sold before, demonstrating effective selling techniques is important. Letting a new person watch you work can be extremely positive training. But let us assume for the moment that you are working with an experienced representative. Why might you go on a sales call?

Take a minute to write down the five most important responsibilities or tasks you perform on a call with your salesperson. Most managers' top response is "To close business." Other common reasons are to "negotiate price" or to "clean up the salesperson's mess."

As we have discussed repeatedly, your job as a sales manager is *not* to sell; it is to *manage* salespeople. You are responsible for coaching, devising strategies, and helping your people build a better motivational environment. There are several problems with going on sales calls if your only objective is to help sell.

Take one of your sales representatives as an example — we will call her Emily. Of the approximately 22 business days in a month, how many will you spend riding with Emily? If you are like most sales managers, you have many other responsibilities and salespeople to manage, and you will be lucky to spend only two or three days each month with her. Dividing 3 into 22, we find that you can accompany her on fewer than 15 percent of her customer calls. Emily is an experienced representative. Although she still needs coaching and training to improve her skills, she already knows how to sell. If you are supposed to sell when you are with her, who does the selling the remaining 85 percent of the time you are not there?

At this point, many sales managers say, "But I only ride with my people on the critical calls. That's when it's important for me to be there." Have you ever told a salesperson that you are going with them on a call because it is just too important for him or her to handle alone? Suppose you accompany Emily on one such call. You, as the more senior (top gun) sales manager, do most of the selling and close the sale. What will happen the next time Emily calls on that customer? He or she will ask, "Where is the *real* salesperson?" Because of your temporary "help" on one call, the customer will consider you the primary salesperson and Emily an assistant from now on.

This is a common trap for inexperienced sales managers and a common problem for salespeople. Many representatives want to know how to get their managers to stop selling on their sales calls.

The Manager's Role on a Sales Call

So, if you are not supposed to sell, what should you do during a sales call? Look at the situation logically. Which will have a more positive long-term impact on a customer: seeing two salespeople wrestling for control of a call, or being introduced to their salesperson's manager as an esteemed client?

Your job is to act like a sales manager in front of the customer. You are not there to sell or negotiate, but to represent your company, and your questions need to reflect this role. Think of long-term rather than short-term objectives. Ask questions such as:

- How has our company been handling your business over the last year?
- Where do you see your company going in the next few years?
- How can we help you get there?

Long-term subjects include discussing the customer's importance to your company. Expressing appreciation for past and continued business is an important function for any sales manager who meets a customer. You also need to reaffirm your company's support and commitment to the long-term customer relationship.

Sales managers can also help collect valuable, in-depth answers to other big-picture questions that affect customer service and competitive advantage, such as:

- What other departments in your company are affected by the types of products or services you buy from us?
- What other products or services would you like to see us offer?
- What did you like most about your previous supplier?
- Being an expert in the market as a buyer, how do we compare with the competition?

- What do you see as our strongest uniqueness?
- What do you like most about our competition?

It is also valid for you to ask, "Why are you being so difficult with our salesperson?" When dealing with troublesome people, you as the sales manager, can take the conversation beyond daily problems and talk about the bigger picture. You can also use questions to break an account "gridlock" that may have formed between your representative and the customer. In these situations, remember to keep your questions focused on the long term. If a customer asks a short-term or single problem-focused question, defer to your salesperson to reinforce that he or she is the one who will ultimately resolve the problem. You may offer statements that demonstrate your awareness and willingness to assist, but it is critical to emphasize that the salesperson is the one the customer needs to deal with on a day-to-day basis and who has the authority to answer such questions.

Above all, avoid the classic mistake of telling the customer, "If you ever need anything, just give me a call." This sends an incredibly clear signal that you are the one in charge, and your salesperson is only a secondary assistant. Try substituting something like the following:

> *Your business is important to us, and we want you to receive the best level of support possible. Your salesperson, Emily, is responsible for your business and what you need from us. She knows more than anyone else in our company about what you're doing, and she'll be able to resolve any problem quicker than anyone. Your satisfaction is important to us. If you have a problem and can't reach Emily, call me. I'm her backup. I might not be able to get you a complete answer immediately, but my staff and I can, without delay, start working on a solution until we can bring Emily and her knowledge of your business situation back into the communications.*

The goal is to reaffirm the customer and their importance to your company. It is also important to show your willingness to help with a problem, as long as they realize that their salesperson is an integral part of any solution. If the customer does call you directly, you can reinforce your representative's importance by having him or her deliver the solution to the customer.

When is it appropriate to jump in and take over a sales call? It is both proper and necessary when you are working with a rookie salesperson. In such cases, you will most likely need to take over from time to time. But you can only take over when the salesperson *gives* it to you. Work out a sign or a key statement in advance that the representative can use if he or she wants you to finish the call. You may also have to step in if your salesperson is sharing information that is illegal, immoral, or misrepresentative of your company's products or services. If you do take over a sales call, you will need to live with the consequences of being involved with that account again in the future.

Your presence can have a valuable strategic impact on a customer relationship if it is planned in advance, used at the proper time, and accomplished without taking power away from your representative who is responsible for the day-to-day selling efforts.

DEBRIEFING MEETING

The debriefing meeting between you and your salesperson following the completed sales call has four goals:

1. *To learn what really happened on the sales call.* If you accompanied the salesperson, get feedback on how he or she thought the call went, what was accomplished, and how your presence affected the customer.

2. *To make sure the salesperson understands what really happened on the call.* Sometimes salespeople are so close to a situation, they miss significant points, opportunities, or problems. You can help increase their awareness by asking questions such as:

   a. What do you think he meant when he said . . . ?

   b. Do you really think our two-week delivery schedule is the reason she's delaying her buying decision?

   Make sure the representative understands the next several steps to take with that customer by asking:

   a. Now that this call is over, what are you going to do before your next visit?

   b. What do you feel needs to be accomplished on your next appointment with this customer?

    c. What do you plan to do over the next several appointments to implement successful longer-term goals and call objectives?

3. *To increase the salesperson's skill awareness.* This is the point at which you encourage them to see how they can enhance their selling skills. Ask questions such as:

    a. How much talking did you do on that call?

    b. How much talking did the customer do?

    c. What could you have done better?

    d. How open were you when the customer described the problems he or she was having with our delivery?

4. *To provide feedback on the selling situation and the salesperson's conduct.* Begin your comments with phrases such as, "This is what I liked most about what you did" or "My overall reaction to how you handled the call was." Keep your feedback balanced — discuss both positives and negatives.

Sales coaching is most successful when it covers all three steps of precall planning, the call itself, and a final debriefing.

RIDE-WITHS

In addition to your sales call coaching, another valuable management coaching and evaluation tool is the "ride-with" or "work-with." We have already talked about accompanying representatives on sales calls, but there are more formalized evaluations of a salesperson's overall selling performance that can be completed when you spend the day with your sales representative. A number of large corporations use managerial ride-withs to evaluate and coach their sales forces.

A ride-with is a situation in which you spend from one to three days riding with a salesperson, coaching, training, and evaluating their overall job performance. Of course, you need to be coaching and training salespeople whenever you ride with them, and you necessarily evaluate their performance through observation of their behavior. But successful ride-withs have a standard set of goals or activities that need to be accomplished during the trip.

Every company tends to define its ride-with goals differently, but some of the most common areas of evaluation and skill-building include the following:

- Observe how effective a salesperson is at communicating and working with customers.
- Examine territory management and calendar organization systems.
- Review year-to-date sales performance numbers and rest-of-year forecasts for the salesperson's complete territory.
- Conduct strategic planning discussions on the most important customers and prospects.
- Review and discuss the representative's annual performance plan progress to date.
- Discuss current product or service offerings, shipping issues, and billing problems.
- Discuss the employee's overall feelings and satisfaction level with the job and the company.

Some companies have managers fill out detailed ride-with reports with copies going to the salesperson and his or her file which is kept by the manager. The main objective is to review a number of important areas with each salesperson in some type of preplanned and consistent manner. Ride-withs allow you to focus on your long-term coaching and evaluation skills. Consider writing a standard set of minimum areas or topics to cover when you ride with a salesperson. Some areas might include the following:

- observations and suggestions to improve the person's selling skills;
- a review of the person's sales forecasts, discussing the accuracy and timeliness of the last several reports;
- a review of the representative's top five or ten accounts with detailed discussions of future goals and plans of action;
- a review of outstanding customer problems with detailed discussions of planned resolutions;
- discussions of territories and business trends you feel might affect either the representative or your company;
- a review of paperwork to see if all orders, forecasts, expense reports,

and weekly call reports are submitted accurately on time;

- discussion of competitive activities and strengths in his or her territory;
- questions about the person's concerns and feelings about you, his or her territory, the job in general, and your company;
- discussion of the long-term issues or directions of your company, customers, and industry; and
- overall strategic territory plans and directions to exceed his or her sales quota.

When you have filled out your form, put a copy in the person's file to help with your year-end performance reviews.

You might already cover a number of these items you would list on a ride-with report. A successful ride-with report serves as a guide or checklist to ensure that you consistently cover all topics or areas on each visit. Ride-with reporting systems provide a consistent implementation process and a way to build an audit trail of your one-on-one discussions with team members.

CRISES

We have established that a major responsibility of an effective sales manager is to make sure the selling environment is strategically focused and to maximize his or her training, leadership, and coaching skills. One of the most critical situations in which you will coach your salespeople comes when you deal with a crisis. We dealt with crisis management in Chapter 2; here we address the difference between a crisis manager and a crisis coach.

A *crisis manager* takes over a problem and personally works toward a solution. A *crisis coach* stays involved in a problem, but makes sure the salesperson handles as much of the work and customer contact as possible. Many managers fall back on top gun tendencies, taking over responsibility for the situation until it is resolved. Although this may lead to quicker solutions in the short run, there can be significant long-term management losses involved with this approach. If you personally handle every problem, how can your people grow and learn? If you coach them now, they will be able to handle the next problem more efficiently, possibly without your help.

Of course, there will still be times when it is best for you to take the lead in problem resolution, for instance, when a salesperson is on vacation or tied up with another problem. You may also be forced to take over if your salesperson contributed to the problem or if the situation is so critical you cannot afford a delay. But these need to be exceptions that occur perhaps once a year. How can you successfully coach your salespeople through "normal" customer crises?

There is an imaginary problem resolution line that most experienced sales representatives learn to identify. It marks the boundary between when they can handle a problem alone and when they need to call in their sales manager. Newer salespeople, having no idea where the line is, tend to call their manager to get involved with every problem that arises. One manager related how she received an emergency call from a rookie salesperson who was standing in a customer's lobby. He wanted her to talk to the customer immediately — he was afraid the customer would be angry because he was delayed in traffic and arrived late for his appointment!

Part of your job as a coach and trainer is to teach your people where the line is *before* problems come up. Walk them through several imaginary or past customer problems. Emphasize that the purpose of the discussion is not to criticize, but to use some real-world problems to show how they could have been handled better. Give your team a five-minute briefing on what happened up to the point at which the situation became a crisis. Next, have the group discuss what could have been done to prevent the problem from occurring at all. What resources could have helped? When would it have been best to get the sales manager involved? Outline when you expect someone to handle a problem alone and when you expect to be informed. Also, make it clear that you are not getting involved to discipline the salesperson but to help keep a customer.

Assume that your salespeople know the proper time to ask for your help. Once you become involved, how do you coach a salesperson successfully through a customer crisis? Consider using the standard steps of a sales call to help the person identify an acceptable solution. You can incorporate these steps with the four stages of crisis management we covered in

Chapter 2. The standard steps of selling are lowering resistance, qualifying the situation, examining and presenting alternatives, seeking closure, and agreeing on the next contact. Think of this in terms of your team. Let us use an example to illustrate the application of these steps to crisis coaching.

For the last two years, you have been coaching Carl, one of your better salespeople, about one of his important prospects. This account could generate a great deal of business if your company can prove its uniqueness and ability to handle the customer's work. Several months ago, you accompanied Carl on a call to the prospect, at which time they seemed interested and asked to test some of your product samples. During a regular territory review meeting, Carl tells you that nothing has been done on the account since the appointment when the samples were promised to the prospect. You are upset with Carl's lack of follow-through on such an important prospect, but your main focus now needs to be coaching him through a plan of action to try to rebuild the selling opportunity.

To *lower Carl's resistance*, briefly tell him how you feel about the situation. Remind him your chief responsibility is to help him solve the problem; you can talk later about what needs to be done to ensure this situation does not happen again. Once you gain a comfort level with Carl, your next step is to *qualify the situation* by asking as many questions as possible. It is normal for salespeople to avoid sharing all information, especially if it pertains to their mistakes. After you have gotten as much information as you can, the third step is to *examine and present solution alternatives.*

As we have stated, the best coaches are those who help their salespeople discover for themselves what the coaches already know. The best way to do this is by asking questions instead of lecturing. In our example, your questions to Carl need to identify what he feels would be the best course of action. Apply his suggestion and, without making any judgment or saying whether you agree, walk him through the possible outcomes of his idea. If the suggestion is not feasible or will not help the situation, it is better for him to realize it himself than to have you tell him it is a bad idea. Keep asking what else can be done until he either gives you an answer you think can work or until he runs out of ideas. If Carl does not develop an acceptable solution, you need to exchange roles and offer him some answers. Ask him to list possible outcomes and consequences of your suggestions. Again, you want him to choose the idea he thinks will work best. Your job is to guide him toward the choice you know has the highest probability of success.

After you have completed all of the potential scenario discussions, the fourth step is to *seek closure*. What actions is Carl going to take? What needs to happen next for him to achieve a positive outcome?

As in any customer sales call, the final step is to *agree on the next contact*. Be sure to discuss when Carl needs to call the customer and when he will update you on his progress.

If you cannot solve a problem through coaching, you may need to become personally involved. Even when you take over, it is still vital that the salesperson stays involved, even if he or she is only observing or working behind the scenes. No matter who handles the situation, it can still be a learning experience for the representative. In this instance, you can keep Carl involved by using him as your coach. Go through the same five steps with him, asking what he thinks should happen at each stage. The point is that even if you are implementing the solution, Carl is learning how to handle future account problems.

After the problem is resolved successfully, it is important to conduct a "problem debriefing" session. This is a meeting with all the people in your company who were involved in the crisis. In our example, this meeting may include only yourself and Carl, or you may ask someone else to assist you with the discussion.

ACCOUNT LOSS REVIEW PROGRAM

Sometimes, no matter what you do, you will still not be able to satisfy your customer and you will lose the business. When you lose a major prospect or existing customer, what happens? In most companies, the answer is nothing. Most salespeople try to forget past losses as quickly as possible. However, a number of larger corporations implement a formal debriefing process called an "account loss review program" to gain insight into the reasons for the loss. The meetings that make up the process are held only for those account losses that management feels significantly affect the company's business revenues or growth.

There are three major goals for these meetings:

1. *To identify what problems and/or trends caused the customer to leave.* If a certain problem resulted in an important loss, it needs to be identified and corrected in other accounts as soon as possible to prevent repetition.

2. *To review and assess the management communications process.* Did the salesperson bring the problem to the sales manager's attention in a timely fashion? Was there enough time to properly plan and implement possible solutions?

3. *To identify any additional training and coaching the salespeople need.* Are your salespeople receiving proper training and coaching to equip them with the skills and insight necessary to handle these types of problems successfully?

A loss review program lets you logically identify exactly what occurred so you can correct the situation immediately and save other selling efforts with the same potential problems. The assumption is that if a salesperson has a certain problem in one account, then he or she will also likely have similar problems developing other accounts. The majority of salespeople treat all of their accounts in an identical manner. Some companies find loss review meetings so valuable that they also hold similar meetings to review significant account *wins*. These discussions help sales representatives see what won the business so they can repeat the behavior. The steps of both types of meetings are basically the same, but we will concentrate on loss reviews because this situation is much more difficult for everyone involved to handle.

A loss review program is not meant to be an inquisition or a disciplinary action. To be effective, these meetings need to be presented as positive evaluation and planning discussions to avoid future problems. They need to be held at least two weeks after the problem has been resolved to let everyone's emotions calm down. These two weeks serve as a "cooling off" period to give everyone involved a chance to look at the incident more logically and objectively.

There are five steps to implementing a successful account loss review program:

1. Announcing the creation of the program
2. Beginning the planning process when a significant selling loss takes place
3. Contacting the customer to learn the details of the situation
4. Conducting the loss review meeting
5. Conducting a separate follow-up meeting to review the sales team's other accounts to ensure none of them have the same loss potential

Announcing the Creation of the Account Loss Review Program

It is important to announce the establishment of your account loss review program before a significant loss occurs. Implementing it after such a loss makes it seem as though you are singling out a specific salesperson.

When you announce the creation of the program to your team, explain why it is important for everyone to learn more about why major accounts are lost to competitors. Emphasize the program's learning potential and downplay any natural disciplinary fears. The problem-solving focus is clear: The more you know about the reasons for problems, the better prepared you can be to prevent them in the future. You do not need to mention that there may be eventual negative consequences and disciplinary actions, which would have happened regardless of the program's implementation. The program's objective is to correct future behavior, not assign blame for past actions.

Beginning the Planning Process

When an important prospect or a large existing customer is lost, you and your management team need to decide if the situation warrants a formal account loss review meeting. If the loss is not significant enough to involve the entire team, you may want to go through the entire account review process informally with your salesperson in a one-on-one setting. Situations that clearly call for a formal review meeting include the following:

- Your company has never dealt with this type of situation before, but it is likely to exist in other customers or territories.
- Additional or different actions could have saved the situation.

- Other departments in the company are involved or contributed to the problem. For example, engineering personnel might need to understand that problems arise when they are late issuing technical specifications.

If the situation warrants a formal meeting, the next step is to have the salesperson involved prepare a written report for the meeting. The report gives your meeting a written focus and agenda. By delegating the creation of the report to the salesperson, you give him or her the opportunity to collect and organize the information he or she will need to be properly prepared for the meeting. Stress that the report needs to be a brief outline, not a 20-page paper. Ask the representative to use the following six questions to generate his or her report:

1. Why did the loss occur?
2. How soon after the account problem arose was the potential for a loss identified?
3. When was management notified?
4. What actions were taken to discover the cause of the problem?
5. What actions were taken to save the account?
6. What could have been done to prevent the problem and the loss of business?

Go over this report with the salesperson before it is distributed so you can coach him or her on the most positive way to present the information and to handle the upcoming meeting. If the report indicates that the problem was due solely to the representative's error, cancel the formal review meeting and deal with the situation in a one-on-one meeting with him or her.

Contacting the Customer

You can handle this part of the process in a private interview or by telephone. Introduce yourself to the customer contact and emphasize your company's gratitude for his or her business and your regret at losing him or her as a valued customer. Then say you hope to get another chance to earn his or her business again in the future. Do not mention the loss review meeting; your goal is to get a fresh view of the situation. You may want to use the following script as a starting point for your call:

Ms. Landreth, it seems we didn't handle our last selling situation with your company as well as we could have. Doing business with you and your company is important to us, and we're sorry we put that relationship in jeopardy. I'm the sales manager responsible for your company. I'd like to ask you some questions about what happened and find out what you think we could have done better.

My goal is to try to correct the problems that occurred so that at some point in the future we might still have the opportunity to do business with you. We want to understand exactly what happened so we can improve our operations and efforts. Your comments will help me better understand the situation and help our company prevent similar incidents in the future.

It is important not to argue with the customer: You are trying to understand the situation, not defend yourself. The customer will be less likely to give you any information if you are on the offensive. Also, in this situation, reality means nothing. All that matters is the customer's perception of reality.

Remember to dig deeper if a customer or salesperson says that price is the reason an account was lost. You do not lose business because of price. If the customer chose a lower-priced supplier, he or she perceived no difference in value, risk, or customer focus between your company and the competitor. To sell against price considerations, you need to make sure the customer understands your company's uniqueness in these three areas. The greater your value differential is, the greater the price differential the customer will accept.

Be sure to end the call by apologizing for any problems your company has caused. Thank the customer for helping you understand what your people could have done differently, and reiterate that you are still interested in working with him or her again in the future. Try saying something like,

Ms. Landreth, I apologize for the way my company handled your situation. It's obvious we caused you a number of problems and a great deal of inconvenience. Thank you for helping me understand what really happened. I'll be working with my people to try to minimize the potential for this problem ever happening again.

I realize this last situation was not handled well, but I still hope that sometime in the future you'll let us show you we've corrected these problems.

Conducting the Loss Review Meeting

It is important that your loss review meeting take place two to four weeks following the loss of business. You need the two-week cooling-off period we have already mentioned, but the meeting needs to be timely enough to ensure that all information is still fresh and that a similar situation could be corrected as soon as possible.

In addition to yourself and the salesperson involved, you may want to invite the director or head of sales (if there is someone over you) or the owner (if your company is relatively small). It is important to include any technical or support people who were directly involved with the account. Remember that people tend to be more honest in their reactions, more willing to participate, and more productive in a small group, so try to limit attendees to fewer than six people.

The meeting agenda is fairly straightforward. The first portion of the meeting consists of the salesperson presenting a brief history of the account, telling who was called on and their titles and importance to the selling decision. The representative also needs to cover the customer's evaluation and decision-making processes. Only 10 to 15 minutes are needed for this portion; you only need some understanding of the customer, not a complete history.

Next, open the meeting to questions from the other participants. The aim is to understand all the reasons the account was lost. Possible questions include the following:

- Did you consider calling someone from engineering to help with the technical support?
- Did the customer tell you their delivery dates were final?
- Did you ask who the competitors were?

Another important goal of the question period is to identify any selling behavior that might have contributed to the loss. Warn your salesperson that he or she probably will not be able to answer all the questions and that it is acceptable to say "I don't know" or "You're right, that probably would have helped."

It is important for you to control the mood and atmosphere of the meeting. You may need to remind everyone that this is a discovery session and not a murder trial. Make sure no one becomes sarcastic or accusatory. Stand up for your salesperson if others become overly aggressive or negative.

Reminding everyone of the meeting's objectives — finding out why the business was lost and identifying what can be done to prevent the same problem in the future — will keep the discussion focused. Although there are many causes for lost business, the following are the most common:

- Inadequate customer contact. Most accounts have only one customer contact. Would calling more people, calling on higher levels, or calling more frequently have helped save the account?
- Incorrect or weak positioning of the company's uniqueness/competitive message.
- Lack of understanding about the customer's real needs and expectations.
- Improper fit between the company and the client. Presentations are sometimes pitched to inappropriate accounts. The more you try to force a fit with the customer, the more likely the account will be open to competitive approaches.

The third portion of the meeting is a discussion of what could have been done to save the account. Could any member of the team have done anything differently? Would involving some of your company's executives or technicians have helped? What needs to change in the salesperson's selling style, customer support behavior, or account strategies to improve your competitiveness? Did he or she ask for help soon enough? What company selling or pricing strategies need to change in order to improve your market advantage? Are you losing business because your competition offers more support or better product quality? Which departments are not reacting to needs or requests completely or soon enough?

After the group has agreed on how and why the account was lost, your final discussion needs to identify other accounts that may face the same potential problems. Does this salesperson have other accounts that are equally vulnerable? Do other sales representatives have accounts that could fall victim to the same situation? If the problem potential is significant, you may want to schedule a meeting with your entire sales team to discuss the situation and outline what they can do to protect their accounts.

It is important to end the loss review meeting on a positive note. Examine possible changes to be made by the entire sales force or management team. What needs to happen for your company to improve its competitive market position and reduce future losses?

Handling the Follow-Up Meeting

Meeting privately with the representative to "debrief" the review meeting is a good time for you to build his or her confidence, since most review meetings are extremely difficult for the salespeople involved. It is also an important opportunity to discuss what changes or actions need to occur to ensure that this problem does not happen with other accounts. What personal changes can the representative make in his or her selling style to reduce the threat of such a situation recurring? What should he or she do differently in communicating with you?

You also need to tell the salesperson truthfully how you feel. Do you think the customer situation got too far out of hand? Did the person make a serious mistake by not following your advice to call on several people? Keep a blend of positive and negative comments to get your message across clearly and help rebuild the salesperson's confidence at the same time.

It is a positive move to include any agreed-on changes from this final meeting in the representative's current employee performance plan. This addition emphasizes the importance of the changes and allows you to track and manage their implementation.

SUMMARY

This chapter has examined the second of the three areas of responsibility you need to improve to successfully manage the selling process: maximizing your sales management leadership, training, and coaching skills. The six situations covered — precall planning, the sales call, debriefing, ride-withs, crises, and account loss reviews — are all vital to your salespeople's (and your) long-term selling success.

The next chapter focuses on helping your salespeople change the way they do their jobs and become more strategically focused for long-term success.

CHAPTER 11

FOCUSING ON THE FUTURE

In Chapter 9, we identified three areas of responsibility in which sales managers need to maximize their skills. We have already discussed strengthening your company's strategic selling focus and coaching and training your sales team. In this chapter, we will talk about helping your salespeople look beyond the next sales call and plan activities that will bring them success during the next quarter or the next year. You will see how to use three important future-focused tools — sales forecasts, commissions and bonus plans, and contests — to their greatest advantage.

COMPREHENSIVE SALES FORECASTING

It is amazing how many organizations do not even ask sales representatives to submit monthly, or even quarterly, sales forecasts. One distributor of hair care products never had salespeople do any forecasting. The vice president said that when the company asked the team for forecasts, the reports were so inaccurate, they were unusable. Forecasting was seen as a waste of time, so management stopped requesting that it be done. This organization, like many others, missed the point of the forecasting process, not to mention ways to improve report accuracy.

Before we look at ways to improve your forecasting efforts, let us take a moment to discuss why salespeople need to perform this task. The most obvious reason for salespeople to prepare monthly sales forecasts is to inform management about sales expectations and how much product will be moved in the next few months. Another reason is to give sales managers an important coaching opportunity. Sales forecasts are excellent tools to identify accounts that may need extra support and/or management attention. The last, and most misunderstood, reason for forecasting is to help sales representatives gain strategic territory awareness.

So, with all these significant benefits, why do the majority of sales forecasts have little to no effect on companies? We talked about the answers to this in Chapter 8:

1. The majority of salespeople see sales forecasts as a waste of time and do not know what purpose the reports serve.
2. Salespeople receive no feedback on their reports once they are submitted to their managers.
3. Most representatives see monthly forecasting as an event rather than an ongoing process. Most are not held accountable for the accuracy of the information presented, so they see no real need to be accurate.
4. Salespeople underestimate forecast numbers to avoid pressure from and look good for management.

How many of these statements apply to your team?

Improving Your Forecasting Efforts

The first step in improving your team's forecasting efforts is to deal with each of the four obstacles listed in the previous section.

First, the sales team needs to understand how sales forecasts are used in your organization. Hold a meeting with your entire sales force and explain the entire sales forecasting process: Tell them how the information is (or needs to be) assembled, show how the completed sales forecasts are reviewed and summarized by you and the management team, and then identify how many other people review the information. Spell out how inaccurate forecasts can cause problems and unnecessary expense for the company. The more they understand how much impact their sales forecasts have, the more effort and accuracy they will invest in them.

Second, salespeople need to receive feedback on the work they do. Even though their paperwork demands are significantly smaller than yours, most salespeople feel they are drowning in it. And why would they devote a great deal of time to a report they will never hear about again? There is a rule of thumb in selling: If you did not hear anything back on your last report, you probably put too much time and energy into it. Do not let your salespeople use this rule. Make sure they know how others in the company benefit from their reports. Hold training sessions on this subject and then maintain the long-term focus by supplying ongoing verbal and written feedback. You can also benefit by evaluating the amount of information you need in a monthly forecast. Streamline the reports wherever possible and eliminate unnecessary requirements that add time rather than substance to the process.

Third, try scoring each of your team member's forecasts. A manufacturer of cleaning chemicals tried this approach to improve its salespeople's inaccurate forecasts. The managers went back through the previous year's forecasts and gave each report two scores. The first counted how many of the clients forecasted actually ordered the chemicals in the month the reports predicted. The average accuracy score for each salesperson was less than 10 percent, meaning only one in ten customers ordered the items at the time the sales representatives anticipated. The second score counted how many companies in the reports actually ordered products within three months of being listed. The average salesperson scored below 50 percent in accuracy here. Consider scoring your people's reports for the past year and tell them that you intend to continue this practice from now on. The scoring system can make them feel more accountable for the information they supply, and knowing that you are keeping track of their numbers will motivate them to put more effort and accuracy into their forecasts.

Fourth, examine your environment to find any factors that might put undue pressure on the sales force. Do the representatives get any kind of feedback on their forecasts? If so, is the majority of that feedback negative? A sales forecast is not a contract, although some managers see them that way. They complain when a salesperson does not close every item listed in the report, so the salesperson avoids listing lower probability accounts for fear of more negative responses from his or her sales manager. Forecasts are meant to be a coaching tool. When you are talking with one of your people about a forecast, it is critical to blend positive and negative comments.

When dealing with inaccurate forecasts, keep in mind that they are only reflections of what salespeople know about their territories: If the forecasts are inaccurate, there is most likely a lack of strategic sales awareness. You can coach your people to use sales forecasts in a strategic territory review. If their strategic focus improves, the accuracy of their information will increase as well.

In Chapter 8, we talked about the three types of information flows — history focused, today focused, and future focused. Salespeople with the most accurate forecasts have the strongest future awareness of their territories. As a coach, you can help your people increase their future focus and improve their view of reality by forcing them to evaluate their territories from a different perspective. You may need to walk some team members through their territory forecasting process.

Newer salespeople, who focus almost completely on historical and current information, will need the most hand-holding in this area. They have no vision of the future and need coaching to improve their overall selling skills. To coach new people on their forecasting skills, use the following steps:

1. Ask them to list all of their current customers, and write the product or service they might sell to this account beside each name.
2. Have them write down the actions they need to take to close each sale and the month or quarter in which they expect the sale to be completed.
3. Prioritize the entire list by closing potential, placing the accounts with the highest probability of closing at the top of the list.

A new salesperson needs to prepare this information before meeting with you. When you meet with him or her, review each account in detail to help assess the accuracy of the person's predictions and upcoming efforts. Offer any additional suggestions that could help him or her increase the odds of closing the sale. Some managers call this *comprehensive sales forecasting* because it identifies everything that might happen in a territory.

Based on all the information, show your salesperson which accounts you think are important enough to be included on a normal monthly forecast. Most rookies do not understand their accounts well enough to accurately identify the timing of a future sale; they also do not know how much guessing you expect them to do on the forecast. Ultimately, you want the person to prepare his or her own forecasts, but until you are comfortable with his or her accuracy, you may want to ask him or her to submit both comprehensive (for your review only) and regular forecasts (for all to see) on a monthly basis. The more you work on his or her selling skills and territory awareness, the more accurate the forecasting will be.

Tracking each sales representative's forecast accuracy is an excellent way to improve your entire team's future focus and territory control. By reviewing the scores for several months' reports, you can show your people how they are progressing. If their scores fluctuate wildly, it is a reliable sign that they have no territory control or future vision of their customers' buying activities and may need coaching help in this area. Increasing awareness is the first and most crucial step to changing behaviors.

One Hundred Percent Forecasting

One way to improve your salespeople's view of their territories is to implement a monthly 100% sales forecasting program. Most representatives have difficulty seeing beyond their next sales call; they have no idea how they will make their quotas for the year. The monthly 100% sales forecast can help them with this dilemma.

What do your people do after you assign them their yearly quotas? In reality, most of them do nothing but complain that their quotas are impossible. Annual forecasts mean little to the majority of salespeople because they cannot visualize what needs to happen during the next 12-month period. So, they ignore their quotas for the first six months, thinking they have the entire year to make their numbers. Right after Labor Day, most of them begin to realize where they are in relation to your expectations and what it will take to meet those expectations. If they are close to making their numbers, they put in the extra effort to successfully complete the year. But if they are nowhere close to making their quota in September, most will give up on this year's quota and not worry about numbers until the following year. Some salespeople have been known to hide orders written in the last two months of the year and submit them during the first month of the new year. Does this sound like anyone on your team?

A monthly 100% sales forecast can help your people visualize their entire year and see what they need to do to make their assigned quotas. Monthly 100% sales forecasts need to be done *in addition to* your normal forecasting process. The normal monthly sales forecast is a more formal document that is reviewed by others within your company. In these reports, salespeople list only those accounts that will actually close within a given time frame. These forecasts are meant as a short-term planning guide and communication document; the goal is accuracy. A monthly 100% sales forecast is more flexible and is meant to be used as a management coaching tool by only you and your sales team. This report identifies what needs to happen for the rest of the year; the goal is visualizing the entire year's selling efforts, and accuracy becomes secondary. With this program, you can help your people see exactly where their sales need to come from during the coming year and target what they have to do to achieve their annual quotas.

Implementation. Implementing a monthly 100% sales forecast program is relatively simple. You may begin at any time, but let us assume you are introducing yours at the beginning of the year. As soon as salespeople receive their annual quotas, ask them to prepare a report detailing how they expect to make these numbers. The worksheet in Exhibit 11.1 is a good form to use for this process.

Assume everyone on your team has an assigned $600,000 sales quota for the year. They need to list the following information on their worksheet:

- Each company to which they expect to sell
- A one- or two-word description of the major products or services to be sold to that account
- The estimated dollar amount of the sale
- The month or quarter in which they expect to close the sale
- The probability of making this sale, listed as a percentage

The information listed here is all you need; any additional facts will only defuse your coaching focus.

Representatives need to make sure their list of accounts and expected dollar sales add up to at least 100% of their sales quota for the year. Although this sounds simple, your people will probably get upset. At the beginning of the year, most salespeople are only able to identify the source of 30 percent to 40 percent of their total sales for the year. If their quota is

$600,000, they will probably only be able to list about $200,000 in forecasted sales. Remember, they are accustomed to developing their normal sales forecasts, in which an account is not listed until it is almost closed. One of the goals of this report is to get salespeople to visualize their entire year and what it will take for them to make their assigned quota.

After they have listed the accounts they *know* they will sell, have them go back and add the names and details of any accounts they have a *chance* of selling. You will most likely need to push them to list accounts that only have a 10-percent chance of closing. Their forecast will probably still not add up to their full sales quota. They may only be able to get up to about $300,000 or $400,000.

Next, ask them to identify the dollar value of their average sale last year. Do not count any big existing customers; try for whatever an average first-year sale would most likely be to a new prospect. For our discussion, we will use $1,000 as an average. To make their forecasts to add up to 100 percent of their assigned quota, the salespeople now need to list how many $1,000 prospects they need to sell during the year to make their numbers. Most completed 100% forecasts usually show about one third of the quota coming from identified customers, another third from accounts listed by name without details, and the final third from "unknown prospects." New salespeople have been known to list over 60 percent of their quota coming from "unknown" accounts.

Once they have completed their forecasts, sit down with them individually to talk about their reports. This is the time for you to ask coaching questions about their territories. Be careful not to get bogged down in the details of any one account. Your goal is to keep them focused on the entire territory for a full year. Ask questions pertaining to each of the major categories on their lists. For the first third of the list, which identifies their known sales opportunities, ask questions like, "What is it going to take to win that order?" or "Do you need any help in planning your strategy for these accounts?" For the second third of the list (long-shot accounts), say, "It's evident you're going to need to sell the majority of these to make your quota. What can you start doing now to begin successfully positioning yourself with these customers?" For the final third, identified as unknown prospects, try starting off with, "It seems realistic to say you need to find a lot more customers if you plan to make your numbers for this year. When are you going to start your prospecting so you can identify enough prospects to make your numbers?"

As you work with your people, emphasize that this is a confidential report. Circulating 100% forecasts could falsely identify accounts as solid opportunities when salespeople have not even called on them. The goal of this report is to get your people to stretch their vision of what it will take for them to make their numbers for the year, not to communicate factual information to other departments in the company.

After the first month of the quota year is over, ask each salesperson to revise their 100% forecast, listing their year-to-date sales on the first line and then updating and balancing the rest of their report so it still adds up to their full sales quota. Each month, you need to also conduct a private coaching session with each salesperson to discuss their reports. The 100% forecast gives you a coaching tool to keep the discussion focused on the entire territory and sales year. Without this report, your representatives will tend to focus only on what they are about to close or whatever is coming up next. A 100% forecast forces your salespeople to view their territories and quota from an annual perspective, and it gives you a way to review their plans and territory strategies on a monthly basis.

Some coaching questions for the first part of the year may be:

- Have you sold any of the big accounts you listed on your first few reports?
- How many of the unknown prospects you listed have you now identified and qualified?
- How have you increased your control and awareness of your territory over the last 30 days?

Toward the end of the year, your questions can change to cover different issues, such as:

- How can you make your quota this year if you still have so many unknown prospects?

- You've been listing the Berkley account as a large sale on every one of your monthly reports so far this year. What do you need to do to get this sold?

Benefits. Companies that institute a monthly 100% sales forecasting program report several significant benefits:

1. Sales representatives begin to actually understand what they need to do to make their quota for the year.

2. Representatives concentrate on the critical need to prospect much earlier in the year. The need to begin looking for new business immediately becomes more urgent to salespeople who list "unknown prospects" for more than half their quota.

3. These forecasts put pressure on sales managers to perform more future-focused coaching. With these forecasts, managers are forced to spend at least some time each month helping their representatives plan and organize the rest of their year.

Most companies find that coming up with enough accounts to complete 100 percent of an assigned quota is a serious stretch for the majority of salespeople. But every once in a while a salesperson easily identifies enough business to fill their list.

Let us look at the example of a company selling specialized replacement valves to large industrial businesses. When this company introduced a monthly 100% sales forecasting concept, one of its sales managers came up with a problem he was not sure how to handle. Because industrial valves is a specialized field, the company had a finite number of accounts in each sales territory. There are only certain types of businesses that can use these products and, even if salespeople did not call on all of these customers, they already knew who these companies were. The majority of salespeople had difficulty thinking of enough accounts to meet 100 percent of their quotas. Most listed a lot of companies they had not even called on yet. But one salesperson, Rita, did just the opposite. When she completed her first 100% forecast, she laughed at how easy it was. She said she had more accounts than she needed.

The managers wondered how to coach Rita and considered three factors:

1. Was Rita's quota high enough? If she had so much potential, perhaps she needed to have a higher quota. This clearly was not the case. Rita had been in her territory for several years. She had only achieved 90 percent of her sales quota the previous year and the coming year's quota had been increased by 15 percent.

2. Were her listing and forecasting efforts accurate? How many of the listed accounts were as strong as Rita thought they were? Her view of potential may have been vastly different from reality.

3. What was Rita working on and where does she need to direct her selling efforts for the year?

After research and discussion, the management team decided Rita had a problem focusing her energies productively. Her territory had so much potential that she was working on too many things at once. She was going after a lot of accounts but not following through on any of them. She was so busy running after new opportunities, she was not closing her outstanding proposals.

During monthly 100% forecast meetings, Rita's manager worked with her to narrow her focus to accounts that had the highest probability of closing. With coaching, her manager also helped her to concentrate on closing existing proposals and not spending so much time going after new bidding opportunities.

By the end of the year, the company's management felt their monthly 100% forecasting program had had a pivotal influence on their success. They felt the monthly coaching sessions had helped focus and guide Rita and the others into more effective territory management habits.

Once your program is in place for several months, you may increase the accuracy of your forecasts by having your people count only the closing probability value of a sale instead of the full amount. For example, if a salesperson lists a $1,000 account as having a 75 percent chance of closing, count that sale potential as $750. A $10,000 account with a 10 percent chance of closing would be counted as a $1,000 sale potential.

Another way you can increase accuracy is to increase the forecast quota number. When a forklift company implemented a monthly 100% forecast program, managers instructed their sales force to use 200 percent of their assigned quota as their goal. Why? The salespeople tended to win about half the proposals they bid on. Making them double their quotas for the sake of forecasting provided a more accurate picture of the work that needed to be done to successfully complete their year. Of course, salespeople also counted their year-to-date sales level twice on their 100% forecast to keep their numbers balanced.

Monthly 100% sales forecasts can give you and your team a more future-focused view of what everyone needs to do to be more successful. If you implement this type of program and build on it, you are building the future of your company, your salespeople, and your own career.

COMMISSIONS AND COMPENSATION PLANS

What type of compensation program does your company currently have in place? Does your current plan allow you to maximize your people and their selling efforts? There are several ways you can compensate your salespeople. Each alternative has positive and negative aspects depending on your selling environment. We will walk through each type of pay plan to help identify which plan is best for you and your company.

Straight Salary

If you pay your sales team a straight salary, you already have an impossible motivational situation. Why would any of your sales representatives sell more than the others if they will receive exactly the same compensation? You will have terrible problems keeping your best people if your top sellers receive nothing extra except your thanks and the potential for a raise next year. Paying a straight salary plus a few thousand dollars in a year-end bonus is not much better.

Some managers say that keeping your job and loyalty to your company should be enough to motivate you, but the reality of selling is that, in almost all cases, it is not. Companies that pay only straight salary watch their best salespeople leave for better compensation packages, whereas poor performers stay forever because there is no financial pressure to improve. The reality is that better salespeople are attracted to the immediate financial payoff for their efforts. In fact, almost all salespeople calculate their personal commissions before they walk out of the customer's door. How much variance in earnings is there between your best and worst salespeople? The less variance there is, the more likely you will lose your best people to better paying companies. As we discuss sales compensation programs, we will assume you have some type of variable compensation in place for your sales force.

Commissions

Many pay plans have significant motivational flaws because sales managers miss the reasoning behind a successful compensation program. Most managers say they pay commissions as a reward for good sales, but this is not the most important reason to pay commissions. The reason you pay commissions is to keep someone selling. Commissions are a future-focus measure, not a history-focused one.

Commission or bonus programs play a major role in your salespeople's motivational environment. If you have a solid, fair commission program, you have the potential to build a strong motivational environment for each of your salespeople. If you have a biased, subjective, or unfair commission program, your motivational environment will suffer profoundly.

This is not just semantics. You pay commissions or bonuses based on the dollar value of what your salespeople sell. But the reasons you pay commissions need to be future-focused to keep your people producing. For example, one national medical supply company sold directly to hospitals and major medical clinics. Each salesperson was assigned a specific geographic territory in the United States or Canada. The problem was that two representatives, one in the Midwest and one in California, had each been pursuing a large hospital contract in their area. The volumes of both proposals were larger than normal, but the buyers swore the representatives to secrecy about the order size. The buyers explained that there was a secret merger pending and the other hospital would eventually be included in the final agreement. Because the manufacturer had little ongoing sales management involvement and coaching, no one at the corporate sales management level knew about the secret bidding situations, and the overlap was missed. By coincidence, both salespeople received a verbal buying agreement from their accounts within the same month. But as the contracts were being drawn up, the hospital merger was announced, and the contract was given exclusively to the Midwest sales representative. The management team was uncertain about how to handle the situation. Both salespeople had worked on their respective hospitals for over a year to earn the business, and there was approximately $20,000 in sales commissions at stake. How would you handle this commission situation?

If you have a history-focused attitude toward commissions, your solution would most likely be to simply split the commission between the two representatives. But what would that do to their personal motivation and job satisfaction? Each put in 100 percent of the effort necessary to close the sale, and each had sold their account in good faith. And because of the verbal agreement, each had already counted on receiving the full $20,000 commission. The company decided to pay the full commission to both representatives even though it severely reduced the sale's profitability to the company. This decision looked at the long-term issue of employee motivation — depending on how long the salespeople stayed resentful (and thus less productive) over the cut in commission, the company could easily have lost ten times the $20,000 they paid in double commissions.

In addition to the straight salary pay plan we discussed earlier, there are four compensation plans that include commissions, and we will look at each of them.

Salary Plus Small Bonuses

Although this plan is slightly better than paying straight salary, it still has some serious flaws. Whenever there is only a small difference between the pay received by your highest and lowest performers, you have a serious motivational problem. Greg, a salesman for an engineering design company, is paid a salary in the low $40,000 range with the opportunity to make a year-end bonus of $3,000 (about 8 percent) if he makes his annual quota. Greg has not made his quota in three years and does not seem to work very many hours. Why? Greg rationalizes his work commitments by dividing his possible $3,000 bonus into the 52 weeks in the year. He identifies that he would receive less than $58 a week for all the extra time and effort he would need to put in to make his quota. As the father of two young children, he feels strongly that the extra time away from them would not be worth the small amount of extra compensation. It does not matter if you disagree with Greg's reasoning and justification. The point of a pay plan is to build a positive motivational environment for each of your people. The salary and small commission Greg receives allows him to justify his work behavior even though his decision is not acceptable to his company.

Think of this from the perspective of a top performer in Greg's company. How motivated would you be if you were outselling and outworking everyone else and you could still only get a $3,000 bonus — the same as everyone else. And because you sell more, that $3,000 is a lower percentage of your value to the company. How long would you, as a top performer, stay with this company? Would you not begin looking for a better-paying opportunity?

The only time this situation is successful is in the case of a straight salary plan that is being moved toward a commission program, in which small bonuses are the first step. But even in these cases, the motivation will wane quickly for your better performers.

Salary Plus Commission or Bonuses

This is the most common pay program used by large corporations. Organizations either pay commissions based on a percentage of total sales, bonuses on units sold, or a percentage of annual assigned quota achieved. Most salary plus commission or bonus plans are balanced so that, in a good year, a salesperson earns less than 40 percent of his or her income in salary. In a poor year, the salary figure will be more than 60 percent.

There are several benefits to a salary plus commission bonus plan:

1. This plan has a positive influence on the motivational environment of the sales force. There is a significant difference in the total incomes of the top and bottom performers — if you sell more, you can earn more.

2. For companies selling "big ticket" products or services, this type of plan evens out the monthly variances in an individual salesperson's paycheck. With this plan, a salesperson can count on a consistent amount of monthly income and at the same time have the potential for an occasional large commission or bonus check.

3. Another benefit of the plan is corporate control. Firms that pay commissions only tend to make their salespeople feel more independent, which affects the way a sales representative reacts to corporate requests and guidance. Most management teams like the idea that they can still influence a salesperson's income by giving raises. When you earn a salary, even if it is only half of your total income, you still tend to listen to the demands of your corporation.

4. A salary plus commission plan is also a "buffered" plan, meaning if you double sales, you do not double the cost of the goods sold. In fact, the more sales increase over several years, the lower your cost of goods sold will become when measured as a percentage of total sales.

As an example, assume you have two direct competitors that sell the same product lines at the same prices with approximately the same profit margins. Company A pays its salespeople on a 100-percent commission pay plan, paying a straight 10-percent commission on all sales. Company B pays its people a salary plus a 5-percent commission on all sales. Compare the total cost of each salesperson to each company as the representatives double their total sales volumes over a five-year period:

	Company A	Company B
Year 1 sales for each salesperson	$1,000,000	$1,000,000
Salary paid	No salary	$50,000
Commission paid	$100,000	$50,000
Year 5 sales for each salesperson	$2,000,000	$2,000,000
Salary paid	No salary	$60,775
Commission paid	$200,000	$100,000

In year 1, each salesperson earned a total income of $100,000 and cost his or her respective company 10 percent of total sales. Compare this to year 5, in which the representatives doubled their annual sales. Assume that company B gave its people a 5-percent raise each year for generating such strong territory sales growth. The $50,000 from year 1 multiplied by a 5-percent raise in years 2 through 5 equals a total salary of $60,775. Thus, in year 5, company A's salespeople earned total incomes of $200,000, still costing the company 10 percent of sales. Company B, however, paid its salespeople $160,775, costing the company only 8 percent of total sales.

Having a pay plan that lowers a company's total cost of sales as the average sales volume per salesperson increases is called a "buffered" pay plan. Under this type of plan, a company actually increases its profitability as a salesperson sells more. Calculated over a 10- or 20-year period, this change in the cost of sales can have a significant impact on the company's profitability. Larger corporations like this plan because of its long-term benefits, whereas small companies tend to dislike it because it increases their short-term risk of carrying a salesperson who may underperform.

Straight Commission

This is the most common pay plan used by small companies. A 100-percent commission plan means that the only compensation your salespeople receive is a commission on whatever they sell. They might also receive some incentive bonuses throughout the year on special promotions or identified products. Many salespeople on these plans pay their own expenses.

For obvious reasons, this plan is most popular with experienced, highly paid salespeople. But there are benefits to the company as well:

1. You know exactly what your cost of goods sold will be for every sale because you pay a specific percentage of each sale as commission. (The most common percentage is 10 percent.) This way, you can always forecast exactly what it is going to cost to sell your products or services.
2. You do not have to carry low producers as part of your sales force. Most companies pay a weekly draw against future commissions to

new salespeople for the first few month of employment, but once the draw is used up, something has to be sold to earn income. Low performers leave on their own without the necessity of being fired.

3. With this plan, it is easy and cheap to add another salesperson. Because you only have to cover the draw for a few months and then pay commissions, you can define the top fixed cost of adding another salesperson.

There are, however, negatives to using this plan. Paying 100-percent commission makes it difficult to attract and develop new salespeople. Because the beginning pay is so low, you will also tend to have a lot of turnover among rookies. There is also the point we mentioned previously: lack of control over salespeople. An experienced salesperson who is paying his or her own expenses will tend to ignore the rest of your company.

Consider, as an example, Kathleen, who owns a company selling office copiers. Due to the company's small size, she also serves as the sales manager for a team of six outside salespeople, all of whom are paid on a straight commission based on gross sales. Kathleen likes the idea of having no "fixed cost" of sales: If sales increase, her salespeople make a lot of money; if sales decline, her sales costs are reduced because the representatives receive less income. She feels this type of pay plan is a good financial fit for her small company, but complains about the difficulties of only paying straight commissions. For example, last month her company added an additional warehouse and repair space to the back of the main building. Kathleen told all employees she needed them to "donate" the next Saturday to help arrange the new warehouse space. Everyone accepted her request, but the salespeople complained, saying they did not feel it was their responsibility. They explained that all the other workers were paid a salary and that part of that salary entailed working extra hours from time to time. Salaried employees could also take extra hours off from time to time and still be paid for the entire week. The salespeople, on the other hand, stated that they were only paid on what they sold. If they took time off, they gave up commissions they would have earned if they were selling. Given this situation, they felt that any extra hours worked needed to be directly related to increasing both their sales and commissions. One of them said, "If you need us to invest an extra weekend working the booth at a business where I can make money selling, no problem. But investing a weekend working at something that isn't going to earn me any extra money is not my job."

Kathleen also found that paying straight commissions tended to make the salespeople feel more independent from her and the rest of the company. Several of them had complained in the past about being asked to participate in extra office-related activities. She felt that the salespeople were beginning to act more like independent distributors or sales agents than her employees. When she challenged them with this, one of them expressed surprise at her attitude since "I don't cost you anything if I don't sell."

What would you do if you were in Kathleen's position? Coaching and one-on-one discussions might help relieve some of the building tension. Increasing her disciplinary tactics might also help establish that she is still in control and that the salespeople have a responsibility to do what is best for the company. But the reality is that paying commissions with no salary tends to communicate a sense of independence and a lack of company commitment to a sales force.

Payment Basis

No single pay plan is the best; all have negative and positive aspects. Deciding on the best compensation plan for your team is difficult. You need to balance what will best motivate your people, what your company can afford, and what your competition is paying.

No matter which plan you use, you need to establish whether payment will be based on gross sales or net profits. It is best to base your decision on whether you want your salespeople to negotiate price with your customers. If you want your people negotiating your selling price, then you want to pay a commission based on profit rather than gross sales. Paying people based on the gross amount of a sale but allowing them to negotiate price means you can lose more than they do when they agree to a lower price.

For example, assume you pay your salespeople a 10-percent commission on gross sales and you have a gross profit margin of 30 percent. If a salesperson cuts the price of a product by 10 percent to close a sale, he or she reduces his or her commission by 10 percent but reduces your profit by a *third*. If you want your people to negotiate price with your customers, make sure that a reduction in price (and your profit) is accompanied by an even greater reduction in their commissions.

Some companies do pay a straight commission based on a percentage of profit, but may restrict other aspects of compensation. For example, one candy distributor pays its sales force a 33-percent commission on all profits generated from their accounts, but the salespeople pay their own expenses.

A number of companies have created a profit commission schedule that identifies the list price and average cost for each item or service sold. In reality, that number is normally the average product cost plus a 10-percent increase to ensure nothing is sold at or below actual cost. The profit schedule also shows the corresponding commission percentage. The salesperson is paid a sliding commission, so a 10-percent reduction from list price could equal a 20-percent reduction in commission and a 20-percent reduction may mean a 50-percent loss of commission. If salespeople can reduce price to make a sale, they need to share in the loss of profit as well. Paying commissions based on profit is a difficult process for your payroll department to track and maintain, but it is necessary if salespeople are to negotiate price.

CONTESTS AND BONUSES

As you evaluate and select the best compensation program for your company, it is critical that salespeople see your plan as balanced, fair, and equitable. Changing a pay plan or commission rate in the middle of the year can cause severe attitudinal problems with your salespeople that could negatively affect their work efforts. You need to make adjustments on an annual basis at the beginning of each year. Once a program starts, changing the rules in the middle can have serious motivational consequences if the changes negatively impact the sales force. Positive changes that increase a salespersons revenue can be changed at any time.

For example, one company sponsored a contest tied to quota performance. Only two of their 15 salespeople had reached their quotas during the previous year. The company decided to raise quotas the next year and initiate a contest where anyone who made at least 100 percent of their quota would earn a one-week Caribbean cruise for two. During the third month of that year, a direct competitor's largest plant burned down. Because of the extra demand this created for their product, all but one of the salespeople made their quotas for the year. Management was livid; they had not expected so many people to qualify when they created the contest. Even though the company made a tremendous profit that year, the owner told the sales force that he had not budgeted for so many people to win, and he was only going to send the top five winners on the cruise. He said he was sure they would understand. He was wrong. Within a year, over half the salespeople who had earned the trip but were not allowed to go left the company and went to work for the competition. The moral here is to be careful of how you manage your contests and bonus programs. A short term savings could have severe long term motivational consequences.

Contests and bonus programs are best used to stimulate short-term enthusiasm and motivation. The longer a contest lasts, the less motivation and improved selling efforts it provides. These programs have to be carefully managed to make sure they do more good than harm.

In Chapter 5, we evaluated whether you used a star or team management approach. We established that the star approach — giving the most time and attention to top performers and ignoring less proficient salespeople — was a less effective method for managing the total sales force. The same is true for contests.

One of the most common mistakes companies make is to design pay programs that reinforce the star philosophy. Does your organization have a "salesperson of the month" contest? Is there a "top salesperson of the year" award? Do you have contests in which the first team member to sell a certain volume wins a bonus? These are all examples of star management. In each case, the contest mentioned can have an extremely negative impact on your motivational environment. The problem is that most contests for salespeople force the representatives to compete directly against each other instead of encouraging them to work together as a team. Animosity between team members can grow to alarming levels. One company had to discontinue its "salesperson of the month" program. The winner was given a parking space beside the front door with a big sign that read, "This car belongs to the top salesperson of the month." The contest was called off because the winners' cars were being scratched by the other salespeople.

If you have a 10-person sales force and hold a monthly "salesperson of the month" contest, you continually (and publicly) identify one representative as a winner and the other nine representatives as losers. The problem becomes even worse if the same few top performers keep winning the contests over and over again. What are the chances the low performers or newer salespeople will try to improve if they feel the same people are going to win every time? Why would you want to have your salespeople compete *against* each other? In worst-case scenarios, this fosters a negative relationship between people working for the same company. Salespeople in some companies that have "top salesperson of the month" contests actually hide sales leads they would have otherwise passed on to another salesperson. Their desire for the award not only reacts negatively on their relationships with coworkers, but on their company's profitability.

The best contests motivate salespeople to sell more without making them adversaries. Every team member has the potential to win, and one person's victory does not eliminate everyone else's ability to earn the same rewards. A contest is successful when over half your people are winners. It is perfectly acceptable to provide monthly listings that rank your salespeople by order of performance: It is important for them to know where they stand in relation to the rest of the team. But you want to avoid bad feelings and infighting over money. You might want to announce that anyone selling over 120 percent of his or her monthly quota this month will receive a specific bonus. Or anyone selling at least ten of your new products this year earns an extra $1,000. These ideas stretch your people without putting them in direct competition with each other.

As a coach you want to be able to talk one-on-one to anyone not winning. With a "team focused" contest, you can tell your salesperson . . . "There was a $1,000.00 bonus check which had your name on it and was waiting for you to achieve your monthly quota. No one took the money away from you. You left the money on the table because you you were not able to achieve your quota. Now let's talk about what you can change or do different this month that might make it easier for you to make your quota."

Creating effective sales contests is a challenge. One company found that the best way to implement a contest was to have the salespeople design it themselves. The team was told how much money they had available and what sales volumes they needed to produce to qualify. From that point, the sales team did all the planning. Management approval was required for the final plan, but the representatives had ownership over their plan. After two years of salespeople-designed contests, the manager says they are still a huge success. Not only have they made the salespeople more productive, they have fostered a feeling of teamwork rather than competition, which contributes to the motivational environment.

SUMMARY

By helping your salespeople improve their future focus, you increase their competitive advantage. Throughout this book, we have looked at what it takes to be a successful sales manager from two perspectives: a focus on building a motivational environment and an emphasis on your job as a coach and guide. The bottom line of all this is: What are you doing to increase your sales team's competitive advantage?

You influence your sales team's competitive advantage through your management style, your involvement as a leader and coach, your ongoing commitment to manage and guide the selling process, your insistence on ongoing sales training for your team, and your willingness to change and grow as a manager and leader. The selling environment and competitive pressures facing your people change every year, and to help them grow and change to meet these pressures, you need to grow and change continually as well.

EXHIBIT 11.1 ONE HUNDRED PERCENT FORECAST WORKSHEET

Date Prepared _____   **Salesperson** _____

Account Name	Major Product or Service to Be Sold	Estimated Dollar Amount Forecasted	Month to Close	Probability of Making Sale (percentage)

Year-to-date performance = $_____
Annual total sales forecasted (total of column 3) = $_____
Assigned annual quota = $_____

Conclusion

How are you going to change or improve as a sales manager now that you have finished this book? Each of us functions in a different environment. If you work in a large corporation, we have covered ideas that may have no relevance to your situation. Many sales managers in large corporations have told us that they do not have the power or the attention of upper management to make any significant changes to their sales teams' selling and motivational environment. On the other hand, if you own or work for a small business, significant changes are probably limited by time and a lack of finances. A number of small business owners have asked us "How can I radically improve my sales management environment when I have a company to run, a weekly payroll to meet, my own customers to sell to, as well as three salespeople to manage?"

All sales managers have justifiable reasons why they cannot or will not change the way they manage their sales force. But if you do not change your sales management style, how can you expect to grow your sales and improve the skills of your people? You have some major decisions to make about ways you can improve your team's motivational environment, ways you can help coach and train your people to more strategically manage their selling process, and ways you can help all your people perform at a higher level than they would have on their own.

Somehow, some way, at some time, someone in your competitive marketplace is going to implement positive changes to their sales management style, the selling success of their sales team, and the strength of their competitive selling advantage. Who is going to be the first to improve their selling success and competitive advantage in your market — you or your competition?

SALES MANAGEMENT FORMS

The forms shown in this appendix are compiled from the exhibits and text examples given in the chapters. All of the forms have been left blank to encourage you to adapt and use them in your improvement efforts.

SALES TEAM DEVELOPMENT PLAN

Overall goals for your sales team in the next 12 months:

_____

_____

_____

_____

_____

_____

_____

_____

Specific training you will give team members to help them achieve these goals and improve their overall performance:

_____

_____

_____

_____

Your team's goals and objectives for the next five years:

_____

_____

_____

_____

Percentage growth in performance each team member will need to achieve these goals five years from now:

_____	_____%
_____	_____%
_____	_____%
_____	_____%
_____	_____%
_____	_____%

SALESPERSON GROWTH AND DEVELOPMENT PLAN

Salesperson: _____

Strengths: _____

_____

_____

_____

_____

Areas that need improvement: _____

_____

_____

_____

_____

_____

Action plan to help this person improve: _____

_____

_____

_____

_____

_____

How you will measure this person's success and growth:_____

_____

_____

_____

_____

_____

_____

BREAKDOWN OF TIME SPENT ON PROACTIVE AND REACTIVE DUTIES

Activity	Real Time Spent	Time Allocation for a Managing Manager
Selling personal customer accounts	_____%	_____%
Prospecting for new customers	_____%	_____%
Processing paperwork and internal bureaucracy	_____%	_____%
Intervening in crises and solving team problems	_____%	_____%
Handling nonsales-related projects	_____%	_____%
Motivating and managing your salespeople and their selling efforts	_____%	_____%
Helping your people with account strategies	_____%	_____%
Talking with your people to ensure their comfort and overall satisfaction with you and your company	_____%	_____%
Coaching your people on account problem resolution	_____%	_____%
Riding with your people to observe and coach their selling skills	_____%	_____%
Providing sales skill training and coaching	_____%	_____%

DETAILED DIARY FOR SALES MANAGERS

Time	Activity
8:00	
8:15	
8:30	
8:45	
9:00	
9:15	
9:30	
9:45	
10:00	
10:15	
10:30	
10:45	
11:00	
11:15	
11:30	
11:45	
12:00	
12:15	
12:30	
12:45	
1:00	
1:15	
1:30	
1:45	
2:00	
2:15	
2:30	
2:45	
3:00	
3:15	

3:30	
3:45	
4:00	
4:15	
4:30	
4:45	
5:00	
5:15	
5:30	
5:45	
6:00	

LEADERSHIP EVALUATION FORM

In order to improve my sales management skills, I need to get your honest opinion of my leadership ability. Please take a few minutes to complete this survey and return it to me as soon as possible. I hope your answers will be honest and candid.

In your opinion, how much of my power is based on my job title?

_____

_____

_____

How much of it comes from my desire to help you grow?

_____

_____

_____

What percentage of my decisions are right? _____ %

What percentage are wrong? _____ %

How important does it seem to me to be right?

_____

_____

_____

How easy is it for me to correct a mistake?

_____

_____

_____

What are the most significant contributions I make to the sales team?

_____

_____

_____

What communication areas could I improve that would have a positive impact on our sales team?

_____

_____

_____

Please add any other comments you have about my leadership style or abilities.

_____

_____

_____

SELF-ESTEEM EVALUATION FORM

Personal Self-Esteem

- How content are you with yourself and who you really are?
- How accepting are you of your following characteristics?
  Weight _____
  Looks _____
  Personality _____
  Relationships _____
  Work achievements _____
  Financial strength _____
- Do you accept yourself as who you are or as what you do?

  _____
  _____
  _____

- How do you feel about yourself overall?

  _____
  _____
  _____
  _____

Managerial Self-Esteem

- How do you relate to and communicate with your people?

  _____
  _____

- How comfortable are you in watching and affirming the success of others in your company?

  _____
  _____

- What do you do to make sure your people are recognized for their accomplishments?

  _____
  _____

- How important is your title to you?

  _____
  _____

- What do you need to re-evaluate or change to increase your success as a sales manager?

  _____
  _____

SAMPLE UNIQUE FACTOR GRADE CARD

1 ·······2·······3·······4 ······**5** ······6·······7·······8·······9 ······**10**

Very Bad   **Neutral**   **Fantastic**

1. How nice a place is this to work?

    _____Coworkers' attitudes toward you

    _____Management's attitude toward you

    _____Customers' attitudes toward you

    _____Service department's attitude toward you

2. How fair is this company?

    _____Fairness of commission plan

    _____Fairness of commission plan administration

    _____Fairness of raises and promotions

    _____Fairness of territory assignments

    _____Fairness of my success potential and future opportunities with
    this company

3. How much potential do I have with this company?

    _____The opportunity to double my income within the next 12 months

    _____The amount of support and help from management in my work

    _____Management's wish for me to be successful and make as much
    money as possible

    _____The company's ability to offer me opportunities to be successful for
    the next 10 years

    _____The opportunity for a promotion path to management

4. What kind of training and selling support do I receive?

    _____Effectiveness of this company's selling and people skill training

    _____Effectiveness of this company's business or industry skill training

    _____Effectiveness of management's support of me and my selling efforts

    _____Effectiveness and cooperation of service department with me and my
    customers

    _____Effectiveness and cooperation of office staff with me and my customers

5. What is this company's impact from my customers' perspective?

_____Effectiveness of our service department

_____Effectiveness of our order entry department and product delivery

_____Effectiveness of our billing and accounts receivable departments

_____Quality of our product line and inventory

_____Uniqueness of our product line

_____Ease of our return policy

_____Effectiveness of our credit department

_____Effectiveness of our pricing

_____Effectiveness of our large customer pricing policies

6. [Add your own questions]

_____**Total**

Employee Performance Plan

Performance Plan for: _____

Begun: _____   **Completed:** _____

Section 1: Business Volumes and Product Objectives

A.   Define minimum quotas
B.   Define expected or require product unit sales
C.   Quantify new account expectations and minimum sales volumes

Plan	Results Achieved	Ranking
A.		
B.		
C.		

Section 1 overall ranking: _____

Section 2: Marketing Objectives

D.   Define proactive selling expectations
E.   Define use of company resources
F.   Identify importance of maintaining and improving customer satisfaction for new and existing customers
G.   Define executive calling expectations

Plan	Results Achieved	Ranking
D.		
E.		
F.		
G. *Internal Company Executives* *External Customer Executives*		

Section 2 overall ranking: _____

Section 3: Territory Management Objectives

H. Define territory boundaries or account assignments
I. Define importance of minimizing lost business
J. Define maximum expense ranges or expectations
K. Define territory reporting systems and information flows required, including forecasts and report deadlines/Define accurate report expectations
L. Define expected productivity and efficiency improvements
M. Minimize levels of outstanding accounts receivable

Plan	Results Achieved	Ranking
H.		
I.		
J.		
K.		
L.		
M.		

Section 3 overall ranking: _____

Section 4: Customer Satisfaction Objectives

N.   Define minimum customer service standards

O.   Identify need for quick customer problem identification and positive resolution

P.   Identify importance of keeping your management team informed and updated on all significant account problems

Plan	Results Achieved	Ranking
N.		
O.		
P.		

Section 4 overall ranking: _____

Section 5: Personal and Professional Development Objectives

Q.   Stress importance of being a team player, positive role model, and professional representative of your company

R.   Identify personal areas to be developed and education plans to facilitate them (Specify skills in the areas of selling, communication, time management, product knowledge, and industry and business knowledge.)

S.   Identify expectations of honesty, ethical behavior, and integrity at all times

Plan	Results Achieved	Ranking
Q.		
R.		
S.		

Section 5 overall ranking: _____

Section 6: Additional Plans and Responsibilities

T.   Identify other behaviors skills, or actions to be worked on

U.   Identify longer-term plans and goals for career development and promotion

Plan	Results Achieved	Ranking
T.		
U.		

Section 6 overall ranking: _____

Summary

OVERALL RATING:

FUTURE-FOCUSED CALL REPORT FORM

WEEKLY CALL REPORT

Name _____

Division _____

Week of _____

Day of Week	Company/Contact Person/title	Plans and Goals for Sales Call	Actual Results from Sales Call

CUSTOMER TELEPHONE OUTLINE QUESTIONNAIRE

Date: _____

Customer: _____

Customer Contact: _____

In this customer's eyes, what makes our company unique?

_____

_____

_____

Why do they buy from us instead of the competition?

_____

_____

_____

What kind of competitive advantage do they think we have?

_____

_____

_____

What are our weaknesses? What exposure could endanger our present or future relationship?

_____

_____

_____

What do we need to do to be more competitive in this market?

_____

_____

_____

Other comments:

_____

_____

_____

Prospect Information Sheet

Date: _____

Prospect _____

Contact: _____

Vendor who won the business: _____

Why did the prospect buy from us?

_____

_____

_____

If the prospect did not buy from us, list the reasons why not.

_____

_____

_____

What did they like (or dislike) about us?

_____

_____

_____

What did they like about our competition? What didn't they like?

_____

_____

_____

What did we do right? (If lost, what did we do wrong?)

_____

_____

_____

What did our competitors do wrong? (If we lost, what did they do right?)

_____

_____

_____

What could we have done better during the sales process?

_____

_____

_____

What did the competition offer that we did not — but that the customer would have liked?

_____

_____

_____

Positioning Worksheet

Based on the results of your questions, to customers and prospects, answer the following questions in detail:

What business are we really in?

_____

_____

_____

What are our customers really buying from us?

_____

_____

_____

Where do we want our company to grow over the next five years?

_____

_____

_____

On which markets or customer industries do we want to focus?

_____

_____

_____

On what product lines do we need to concentrate to maximize profits?

_____

_____

_____

What is our competitive advantage?

_____

_____

_____

How are we competitively positioned?

_____

_____

_____

What can we do to showcase our uniqueness?

_____

_____

_____

COMPETITIVE MESSAGE WORKSHEET

Why is our company unique?

_____

_____

_____

What value does our company offer that others do not?

_____

_____

_____

What "philosophy" is behind this value?

_____

_____

_____

How can we position our company's message to prove our value differential?

_____

_____

_____

Our new message is:

_____

_____

_____

ONE HUNDRED-PERCENT FORECAST WORKSHEET

Date Prepared _____   **Salesperson** _____

Account Name	Major Product or Service to Be Sold	Estimated Dollar Amount Forecasted	Month to Close	Probability of Making Sale (percentage)

Year-to-date performance = $_____
Annual total sales forecasted (total of column 3) = $_____
Assigned annual quota = $_____

Index

Dartnell's Sales Tools to Motivate, Inform, and Empower

The Idea-a-Day Guide to Super Selling and Customer Service

by Tony Alessandra, Ph.D., Gregg Baron, and Gary Couture

Set your goals even higher — and reach them! Start each workday with a 15-minute session with this personal sales "trainer," and you'll find yourself overcoming your selling weaknesses, shoring up your strengths, and learning new techniques. You choose how to use this skill-building tool: build good sales habits day by day; read the carefully organized sections as you need to reinforce specific areas; or do both at once. Fifteen sections include 250 hard-hitting ideas, as well as handy checklists, information sources, worksheets, and a self-diagnostic test, all designed to keep you on the road to success.

320 pages; paperback; $19.95; Book code: 1185

Sales Promotion Handbook, 8th Edition

Edited by Tamara Brezen Block and William A. Robinson

More than 30 of the world's leading sales promotion authorities share their marketing wisdom in this all-new edition of the industry bible. Timely topics include:
- Developing plans and strategies for optimum success;
- Integrating sales promotions into the marketing mix;
- Promotion in the global marketplace.

910 pages; hardcover; $69.95; Book code: 1212

Questions That Make the Sale

by William Bethel

Propel your sales to ever-higher levels by asking the right questions. Eleven information-packed chapters show you how to:
- Rivet attention on your presentations;
- Identify and clarify your customers and their needs;
- Motivate, qualify, prospect, probe, and close with greater success.

The final chapter contains 365 questions ("a question a day") to achieve greater sales success.

198 pages; paperback; $19.95; Book code: 1196

Sales Manager's Handbook

by John Steinbrink

The bible of the industry, this highly regarded handbook provides sales managers with the timely information, detailed case studies, and solid techniques they need in order to make wise decisions. And everyone in your sales office can use this book as a quick, easy-to-understand reference for finding an information source; creating documents, forms, and plans; and much more. Includes how to:
- Compensate and motivate your staff;
- Manage a sales function;
- Plan and run productive meetings;
- Plan overall strategy;
- Hire and train a quality staff.

1,272 pages; hardcover; $49.95; Book code: 1162

Performance Driven Sales Management

BY GEORGE S. ODIORNE

Manage your sales force more profitably with this step-by-step management guide
- Set realistic profit and performance goals;
- Develop team-driven sales goals and strategies;
- Measure progress fairly and accurately;
- Train for maximum effectiveness.

An 80-page "Sales Management Workshop" shows these ideas in action in real-l
situations.

260-page text; 80-page "Sales Management Workshop"; 3-ring binder; $91.50; Book code: 1189

YES, Send me the book(s) I have checked. I understand that if I am not completely satisfied, I ma
return the book(s) within 30 days for a full refund.

____ **THE IDEA-A-DAY GUIDE TO SUPER SELLING AND CUSTOMER SERVICE**; $19.95; Book code: 1185

____ **SALES PROMOTION HANDBOOK, 8TH EDITION**; $69.95; Book code: 1212

____ **QUESTIONS THAT MAKE THE SALE**; $19.95; Book code: 1196

____ **SALES MANAGER'S HANDBOOK**; $49.95; Book code: 1162

____ **PERFORMANCE DRIVEN SALES MANAGEMENT**; $91.50; Book code: 1189

Bill my: ☐ VISA   ☐ American Express   ☐ MasterCard   ☐ Company

Card Number _____ Exp. Date _____

Name _____

Title _____

Company _____

Address _____

City/State/Zip _____

Signature _____ Phone (____) _____

(Signature and phone necessary to process order.)   95-5503

Copies may be ordered from your bookseller or from Dartnell.
To order from Dartnell, call toll free **(800) 621-5463** or fax us your order **(800) 327-8635**.

☐ Please send me your latest catalog.

DARTNELL
4 6 6 0   N   R A V E N S W O O D   A V E ,   C H I C A G O ,   I L   6 0 6 4 0 - 4 5 9